SURVIVING
DENALI

THE AAC PRESS

NEW YORK

S U R V I V I N G

A Study of Accidents on Mount McKinley
1903–1990

Second Edition, Revised

JONATHAN WATERMAN
CHAPTER ON MOUNTAIN MEDICINE BY PETER H. HACKETT, M.D.

ISBN 0-930410-48-3

Manufactured in the United States of America

Published by The AAC Press
113 East 90th Street, New York, New York 10128-1589
The AAC Press is an Imprint of The American Alpine Club, Inc.

The American Alpine Club, Inc. was founded in 1902 and began publishing in 1907.
It is dedicated to the promotion and dissemination of knowledge pertaining to
mountains and the art of mountaineering in all of its forms.

Book Design by Carol Malcolm-Russo

Graphs by Coghill Composition, Inc.

Text composed by Coghill Composition, Inc.

Title Page photograph by Bradford Washburn

Permission to reprint copyrighted material is
acknowledged: p. 1, © Howard N. Snyder 1973.

TO CHRIS AND HIS COURAGE

WHY DENALI?

The State of Alaska Board of Geographic Names now refers to Mount McKinley as *Denali,* the original Indian name for the peak, which means *The High One.* In 1896, a prospector, ignorant of native traditions, named the mountain for William McKinley, the Republican presidential candidate of the day. The Federal Government still retains the name *Mount McKinley,* although the National Park lands which encompass the mountain were renamed *Denali National Park and Preserve* in 1980. Except in quoted material, this book uses the name *Denali* throughout.

The mountain lies at latitude 63 degrees north, 390 kilometers from the Arctic Circle, and is 6,194 meters (20,320 feet) high.

ACKNOWLEDGMENTS

For all their time and invaluable perspectives, my special thanks to: Bob Gerhard, Bob Seibert, Debbie Frauson, Roger Robinson, Tom Griffiths, and Scott Gill, all of Denali National Park and Preserve.

I would also like to thank: Sindy Ernst, Mike Kennedy, Tom Schwarm, Brian Okonek, Glenn Randall, Ralph Bovard, Dave Buchanan, Rod Newcomb, Bradford Washburn, Charles S. Houston, Chip Woodland, and Peter Hackett for their patient review of the manuscript and for their insights.

For generously contributing photographs, I am grateful to: Dave Buchanan, Mike Covington, Scott Gill, Mike Graber, Gary Kofinas, Art Mannix, Holm Neumann, Brian Okonek, Glenn Randall, Roger Robinson, Kathy Sullivan, Jack Tackle, Ian Wade, and Jed Williamson.

And thanks to Patricia Fletcher and Franc de la Vega for their patient prompting and editorial advice.

These selfless people—rangers, climbers, guides, writers, photographers, teachers, doctors, editors, and friends—all know the meaning of service to the climbing community.

PREFACE

My ongoing involvement with Denali started in 1982, at the invitation of Bob Gerhard, who was then the Mountaineering Ranger. He was concerned about the high number of rescues, deaths and cold injuries on the mountain in the late seventies. Since I was interested in doing high-altitude medical research on the mountain, we were able to establish and operate a camp at 14,300 feet on the West Buttress.

Over the past nine years, the Denali Medical Research Project and the National Park Service, working together, have markedly reduced altitude illness, frostbite, and deaths and rescues on the mountain. During that time, Jonathan Waterman also logged many months on the mountain, guiding and climbing for fun, and working as a ranger. Subsequently, as we worked together on many rescues, I gained increasing respect for his capabilities and insights. We often reflected on the situation on Denali, marvelling that so many of the people attempting the mountain really had no idea of the level of commitment required.

The motivation for writing this book is to dispel the myth of Denali as a cakewalk, and to help climbers prepare adequately for polar, high-altitude survival. By learning from the past, climbers can avoid similar problems in the future; this is the goal of *Surviving Denali*. Waterman presents an in-depth analysis of altitude medical problems, frostbite, avalanche and fall injuries, and deaths on the mountain in order to point out the mistakes that may have been made and methods that might have been used to prevent them. His focus is not morbid curiosity, but to provide a true learning experience for the climbing community. In fact, the climbers attempting Denali seem to be more sophisticated each year; in part, perhaps, due to the first edition of his book.

Nonetheless, *The High One* remains unique among the mountains of the world. Situated at latitude 63 N, it is the highest point near the Arctic Circle. Piercing the central plain of Alaska, Denali is buffeted by storms from the gulf of Alaska and from the Bering Sea. In few mountain locales of the world does the weather change so precipitously and dramatically. A balmy day of glacier travel can rapidly deteriorate into a day of survival-snow-cave digging. The intense cold is, of course, another unique feature of Denali, comparable only to the Antarctic ranges. The Himalaya is tropical by comparison. On the South Col of Mount Everest (26,200 feet) in late October, the lowest temperature we recorded in 1981 was 17 degrees below zero. On Denali, this would be a rather warm night at only 14,300 feet in May and June. Temperatures between the high camp and the summit even in the middle of summer, are routinely 20 to 40 degrees below and even lower at night. This combination of extreme weather and temperatures pummels the unprepared.

Denali also renders the climber more hypoxic; the barometric pressure is lower for a given altitude than on mountains closer to the equator. This difference becomes noticeable above 10,000 feet or so, and it makes the summit of Denali equivalent to anywhere from 21,000 to 23,000 feet in the Himalaya (Mount Everest is at latitude 27 N), depending upon weather conditions. The barometric pressure is also much lower in the winter than in the summer. Lower barometric pressure means less oxygen in the air; therefore Denali is more of a hypoxic stress and physiological challenge than one might expect for its altitude.

Because of these unique features, climbers on Denali often are pressed to survive. The fact that the West Buttress route is not technically difficult should not obscure the need to plan for extreme survival situations. Of course, some climbers manage to get up and down in a perfectly nice, but rare period of weather; when back home, they encourage others to climb this "easy walkup" of a mountain. Little do they realize that it was only by sheer good luck they weren't trying to keep their tent up in the middle of the night in a 60-mph wind at 40 degrees below zero, with boots on and ice ax ready in case the tent suddenly imploded. Because of the nontechnical reputation of the popular West Buttress route, it is a terribly underestimated climb.

Despite this, there are still many for whom Denali is the next step after Mount Rainier or Mount Hood or Longs Peak. Much better "warm-up" climbs for Denali would be winter ascents of these peaks or, perhaps, a winter ascent of Mount Washington. There is, of course, no place in the continental United States to truly experience the altitudes encountered on Denali. Proper preparation, knowledge of acclimatization, and the ability to recognize mountain sickness, especially pulmonary edema, will help climbers to survive. Proper training, adequate equipment and knowledge of winter survival skills are also essential. *Surviving Denali* is a must for every climber considering an attempt on *The High One*.

PETER H. HACKETT, M.D.

CONTENTS

INTRODUCTION

Denali is the coldest, highest mountain in North America. Hardcore alpinists, mountaineers, rock climbers, and neophyte backpackers flock from every country in the world to pit themselves against the mountain. Although most of these people succeed, too many others fail because of the cold, altitude sickness, falls, avalanches, storms, or their own negligence. Accidents on the mountain are common.

Since the 1983 edition of this book was published, traffic on Denali has increased steadily. Major changes have been implemented to stem the tide of unnecessary accidents and ease the environmental impact of so many climbers. For one, Peter Hackett's High Latitude Medical Research Camp has undoubted saved many lives. The National Park Service has increased ranger patrols, and encouraged safe and environmentally sound climbing practices. It also presents a helpful multilingual slide show to climbers checking in at the Talkeetna Ranger Station.

Nonetheless, certain types of accidents are on the rise. Soloing, for one, has become more popular, resulting in an increased number of crevasse falls and mystifying disappearances. Sick climbers have been abandoned while the remainder of the team goes to the summit—a most disturbing trend. Carbon monoxide poisoning (from cooking in sealed tents or snow caves) has resulted in at least two deaths and many more cases of pulmonary edema. And the surge of winter climbing accounts for the prevalence of frostbite, as well as the highest death rate for any season or category of climbers on Denali. Foreign climbers, while constituting only a small percentage of the total numbers, have accounted for the largest percentage of accidents. For instance, Europeans often climb too fast to acclimatize. Germans have fallen from Denali Pass because of their refusal to use ice axes; Koreans have been involved in four noteworthy accidents (and rescues) on the Cassin Ridge in a period of four years. Last, but not least, Americans have had their problems as well. In particular, guided parties have fallen off or been blown off (while inside their tents) the ridge crest of the West Buttress.

Long-time accident patterns continue to recur with frustrating regularity. Frostbite continues to plague up to half of those who climb from February through May. Recent statistics show that June and July attempts are more successful, warmer, and less likely to induce frostbite. Parties blithely continue to camp in the 12,500-foot West Buttress basin and to get buried in avalanches—miraculously, no one has died. Finally, unnecessary helicopter rescues still occur, due to a general lack of self-sufficiency and guided party mishaps.

Mainly because of expensive helicopter usage, rescue costs on Denali exceed those of any other single mountain-rescue operation in the country. Although the costs are small compared to taxpayer dollars spent by the Coast Guard or the Federal Aviation Administration for boat and aircraft rescues, climbers must take more responsibility. A 1986 rescue of two Koreans on the Cassin Ridge cost $23,141.

If rescues increase, climbers may eventually have to post bonds to cover potential rescue costs. Many climbers have insurance coverage, but in recent years the Park Service has developed a policy of not billing victims for rescue costs. Despite the government's lack of progress and dynamism, many victims and their families have begun making donations to upgrade the Talkeetna Ranger Station's rescue capabilities.

Although helicopter rescues have undoubtedly saved many lives on Denali, the availability of "free" helicopters has inadvertently encouraged a lack of self-reliance and has interrupted the wilderness ethic on the mountain. The medical research camp, although needed, has also unintentionally contributed to a false sense of security among climbers. Certainly, one would hope that studying the accident patterns within this book would help to avert needless tragedy and risk imposed on rescuers, as well as emphasizing the need for proper self-sufficiency and respect for the mountain.

Surviving Denali presents a series of accident narratives together with specific recommendations on how to safely climb the mountain. As it is impossible to describe every accident, only the most documented or potentially educational episodes have been included. I have also included many rescues and near misses in which I was involved as a climber, ranger and guide during the period from 1976 to 1987. Although my own hands-on involvement might lack objectivity, both the immediacy and insight I have gained needs to be shared. *Surviving Denali* is not a scientific or medical treatise (nonetheless many physicians have reviewed and commented upon the text). For further information, a bibliography and appendices are included. Ultimately, no book can substitute for the judgment, skill and intuition gained from experience.

In many instances, such as when frostbite occurs, victims either take care of themselves or are evacuated quietly by their own team. Although self-evacuations are seldom reported, they do represent the most exemplary kind of behavior on Denali. There is considerably more documentation on the big, costly rescues involving climbers who lacked the necessary experience or were not able to take care of themselves. When known, the rescue costs are noted in the summaries at the end of each chapter. (The omission of rescue costs indicates that complete information was not available.) Although accidents in other areas of the Alaska Range are excluded, the text is applicable to big peaks throughout Alaska and the Yukon Territory.

Reviewing accidents does have its limitations. In particular, hindsight often seems harsh in light of the fact that every climber "screws up." There are also accidents involving objective dangers that can be attributed to bad luck. Then, too, it is not possible for all accidents to be prevented in this game of sought-after risk. But surely, climbers can reduce objective dangers and risk taking by studying the following anecdotes and learning from the mistakes of others. More importantly, be careful.

SURVIVING

DENALI

C H A P T E R

O N E

The Self-Sufficient Pioneers
1903–1967

Alone, their last desperate chance
now gone, the men relinquished
the fragile thread of life.

Howard Snyder in
THE HALL OF THE MOUNTAIN KING

Denali *was the unknown mountain. Men spoke of it* in hushed, reverent tones. Consequently, the early climbers were willing to risk life and limb for North America's highest peak. There were no rescue teams and no helicopters; equipment was primitive and very little was known about high-altitude sickness, rope technique, avalanches or first aid. Self-sufficiency, a concept alien to many modern climbers, was their tool for survival.

Nearly all climbers on Denali—particularly the pioneers— have found their limits. Given the arctic cold, storms and altitude, it is easy to overextend oneself; of the early climbers, 5.9 percent were involved in accidents. This figure is more than twice the rate for recent (1967–90) climbs on Denali. In the early years, climbing the peak was considered an outrageous achievement. After all, Denali was unknown and had an almost malevolent mystique. What the early climbers lacked in knowledge and equipment, they made up for in self-sufficiency and perseverance; some paid an eternal price.

In a one-day summit bid in 1910, four plucky "sourdough" miners carried double-bit axes and a 14-foot spruce pole for 8,000 feet to the north summit of Denali. They made no mention of altitude sickness and considered ropes to be unnecessary. They ate doughnuts, steaks and stew.

Three years later, Hudson Stuck, Archdeacon of the Yukon, and his party made the first ascent of the higher, south summit. The night before the attempt, they lay sleepless with indigestion. After they started up, Stuck wrote, "We were rather a sorry company. Karstens still had internal pains; Tatum and I had severe headaches. Walter was the only one feeling entirely himself." Stuck "had almost to be hauled up the last few feet, and fell unconscious for a moment upon the floor of the little snow basin that occupies the top of the mountain. . . ."

After the first ascent, no one would attempt the mountain for 19 years. Then, in 1932, two parties arrived. The first, led by McKinley Park Superintendent Harry J. Liek, was brought to the Muldrow Glacier by dog sled. From here, they climbed both the north and south peaks.

The second party, the Cosmic Ray Expedition, was flown onto the lower Muldrow Glacier. Allen Carpé and Theodore Koven started up the route on skis, taking scientific light measurements. The rest of the party, Nicholas Spadavecchia, Percy Olton and Edward P. Beckwith, stayed behind. When Beckwith became ill with ptomaine poisoning, Spadavecchia hiked out to get help from Fairbanks.

Carpé and Koven, meanwhile, grew concerned about the others and started back down the glacier unroped. Apparently, Carpé traveled behind Koven on foot and fell into a crevasse. When Koven returned on skis to help, he fell into the same crevasse. Although he managed to climb back out, he bled to death in the cold.

Two days later, the descending National Park Service party found Koven's body on the glacier, but couldn't find Carpé's. They set off down the glacier, hauling Koven's body with a climbing rope. One member of the party, Grant Pearson, was unroped and fell into a crevasse, but climbed out with only facial lacerations.

Liek's party broke the news to Olton and the ailing Beckwith and continued down to Wonder Lake. Liek also notified the Park Rangers that Spadavecchia was lost; he was later found at McGonagall Pass. Olton and Spadavecchia walked out with the rangers, while Beckwith was evacuated by airplane from the Muldrow Glacier.

Although not common, crevasse falls would occur again in later years.

In 1951, Bradford Washburn pioneered the West Buttress route with the support of airdrops and blazed the easiest way for the thousands of climbers to follow. His painstaking photography of the mountain would also inspire numerous new routes.

The first reported frostbite accident occurred in 1953, when Andres Henning suffered frostbitten feet while carrying loads up Karstens Ridge on the Muldrow Glacier route. Although he carried insulated felt boots, he was climbing in leather boots. When his feet turned black, his party descended to the McKinley River; he was then flown out to Wonder Lake by a survey helicopter. Park Ranger Elton Thayer drove Henning out of the park.

The next year (1954), Thayer led a bold first ascent of the South Buttress. After reaching the summit, the party of four then started down the Muldrow Glacier route. In order to safeguard the steep Karstens Ridge, Thayer traveled last because the group was tired and ice-ax belays were difficult in the rotten snow conditions. As he skirted the ridge crest, Thayer slipped, pulling his companions 900 feet before one member of the group fell into a crevasse and stopped the fall. Thayer died from a broken neck and George Argus broke his hip. The two remaining climbers left Argus with all of the provisions and hiked out to Kantishna to get help.

Six days later, a helicopter dropped a seven-man rescue team at 6,000 feet, the highest landing yet made on Denali. They carried Argus on a litter to McGonagall Pass; from there, he was evacuated by helicopter. This was the first rescue team on the mountain. In time, as more climbers came, self-sufficiency was forgotten, helicopters flew higher and higher, and rescues became commonplace.

Aircraft began to play an increasingly important role on the mountain. Airplanes and helicopters have been associated with every climb since the tragic Cosmic Ray Expedition. Washburn returned and shot aerial photographs of the mountain. However, flying near the mountain was chancy and involved more vagaries and downdrafts than the primitive crafts could handle. Wreckage littered the mountain.

In 1944, and again in 1952, military plane crashes on the glaciers east of Denali accounted for 38 deaths. Fred Beckey's 1954 Northwest Buttress team—inspired by Washburn's photographs—was supported by airdrops. Their plane, however, was forced onto the Peters Glacier and destroyed in high winds. In 1959, Washburn's aerial photography prompted still another team to climb the central bulge of the South Face, later named the West Rib.

In these years, airplanes also played an important role in the exploration of the isolated Alaskan bush; thus the drone of engines became part of Denali's history. Aviation technology, hand-held radios and the mountain's increasing popularity made for more and more rescues. Eventually, the National Park

6

Service evaluated each team's experience before permission to climb was granted.

In 1960, an epic air and land rescue showed how far reaching the consequences of an accident could be. On May 14, a four-man expedition landed at 10,200 feet on the Kahiltna Glacier. Lou and Jim Whittaker (who would later be the first American to climb Everest) led the climb. Peter Schoening had been on two major Himalayan expeditions and John Day had trained on 14,000-foot peaks in Colorado. The group reached the summit in three days from their base camp. (In later years, climbers repeatedly contracted altitude sickness on such speedy climbs. However, a few climbers, like the sourdoughs, actually beat altitude sickness by climbing up and down in one day.) During the descent below Denali Pass, someone slipped—possibly due to altitude sickness—and pulled all four 400 feet down. Day injured his leg, while Schoening and Jim Whittaker were briefly knocked unconscious. Paul Crews, who was with another team, set up a tent over Day while Schoening and the Whittakers descended to 16,800 feet. They used Crews' radio to call for help and a 50-man rescue team from Alaska, Washington and Oregon was mobilized. Meanwhile, Helga Bading, a member of Crews' party, contracted pulmonary edema at 16,400 feet.

The next day, a sled and food were airdropped at 17,200 feet and Bading was lowered to 14,300 feet where Don Sheldon made a record-breaking glacier landing and evacuated her. Farther down the mountain, an experimental helicopter crash landed on the glacier in a whiteout and a strut ripped through the cabin, narrowly missing the heads of the rescuers. On May 20, an observer plane crashed and burned a short distance from Day's tent. Both the pilot and the passenger were killed.

Schoening was still dazed and suffering from frostbite, the Whittaker twins had mild frostbite; and, although Day's condi-

Self-sufficiency was superceded by radios, helicopters, and dependence on other climbers. *ART MANNIX*

tion was stable, he needed an airlift. On the evening of the 20th, pilot Link Luckett stripped the battery, doors and all but 15 minutes of fuel from his chopper. He then made a "controlled" crash landing at 17,200 feet. Day was loaded in and whisked down to another plane at 10,800 feet. Luckett plucked Schoening off the mountain the next morning.

The repercussions were widespread. A group of Japanese in the path of the rescue were flown off the mountain. The weather, which had been cooperative, soured. Three days later, when conditions improved, Sheldon flew to 14,300 feet to evacuate a rescuer with pulmonary edema (unacclimatized rescuers were seldom used again). The ordeal became front-page news around the country and for weeks after the rescue, climbers on the West Buttress dined on leftover sake and airdropped food inside abandoned Army rescue tents.

As the mountain's reputation grew, its mystique diminished, thus setting a precedent for rescues. The word leaked out that if you were in trouble on Denali, you could be rescued. The days of the self-reliant sourdough became history. In 1960, out of 24 attempts, 23 climbers were successful (the previous year, four out of eight climbers reached the summit). The number of climbers increased as climbing North America's highest mountain was seen as a feather in one's cap. Guided parties tested the waters, and new routes continued to be sought after. Boldness, however, exacted a toll on the mountain with the worst weather in the world; during the sixties, one out of every ten climbers was evacuated and 3.1 percent were killed.

Riccardo Cassin read Washburn's description of the greatest problem left on Denali, and the photograph of the South Face was enough to convince the Himalayan veteran to lead a climbing team to the mountain. In 1961, they flew over from Italy to attempt the unclimbed Cassin Ridge. After several weeks of climbing, Jack Canali's feet were frostbitten during a gale on the summit day. On the descent, he couldn't fit his swollen feet into his boots, so another team member sacrificed his; Canali made a painful and dangerous retreat without crampons. Two days later, Sheldon flew three of the Italians to the hospital for frostbite treatment: no toes were lost. President Kennedy cabled congratulations to Cassin for "This outstanding accomplishment under the most hazardous of conditions. . . ."

Meanwhile, on the more popular West Buttress route, frostbite became common. Sometimes, getting to the top overrode concerns of the flesh, and climbers would stagger up in atrocious weather conditions. In 1960, one climber frostbit his fingers while trying to don his face mask in eight-mph winds at 19,500 feet. Two members of a Canadian group froze (and later lost all of) their toes on a cold summit day. Elsewhere, a British climber cinched his crampon straps too tight while going to the summit and frostbit his big toe. (Two members of the same group experienced snowblindness as a result of inadequate amber sunglasses.) Another climber, wearing poorly insulated boots with the laces too tight, froze his foot while approaching the summit.

In 1963, after the first ascent of the dangerous Wickersham Wall by a Canadian team, Hans Gmoser said, "I do not consider it safe and I have no desire whatsoever to repeat the climb, fully aware that it was only due to lucky circumstances that we were able successfully to complete our trip". (1964, *American Alpine Journal*.) During their descent of the West Buttress, they skied past a Rainier Guide Service group wading in hip- to chest-deep snow. One of the clients, who was breaking trail, suffered frostbite because his feet were continually submerged in the subzero, beneath-the-surface snow. Thirty-three days after the Canadian Wickersham Wall climb, a Harvard team completed a more difficult route on the wall. As of 1991, the route has not been repeated due to frequent rockfall and avalanche dangers.

That same year, another Canadian climber frostnipped his fingers while fixing a stove. Then, while digging a cave at 12,800 feet, his mittens got wet. Later the mittens froze and his fingers became frostbitten.

Although frostbite injuries on Denali could be attributed solely to the arctic weather conditions, dehydration, poor diet and altitude sickness are probably the prime causes; sometimes faulty equipment is to blame.

In the winter of 1967, eight self-sufficient, experienced Alaska Range climbers proved that frostbite can be minimized, if not prevented. The climbers wore white vapor barrier or "mouse" boots and built igloos to escape the cold and wind. Disaster struck on the third day when Jacques Batkin fell 50 feet into a crevasse and died of head and chest injuries. He had been traveling unroped, without skis or snowshoes, which might have prevented him from falling into the crevasse. Although another member of the group had fallen into the same crevasse earlier on the climb, the hole was left unwanded. Sheldon flew the body out and the group continued—albeit halfheartedly—in Batkin's memory.

Johnston, Davidson and Genet reached the summit on March 1. They bivouacked at Denali Pass, pinned down by high winds for the next week with little food and water. Eventually, they dug a cave and found some fuel which Johnston had cached several years before, both of which saved their lives. The rest of the team assumed that the trio had died in the windstorm. After the wind abated, an air search was organized. When the three climbers started down, their frostbite was relatively minor, a testimony to their vapor barrier boots and to their caving instincts at Denali Pass. Despite their initial protests, Johnston,

12

Davidson and Genet were picked up at 13,150 feet by a helicopter. Such an overreaction was a portent of the years to come. The number of rescues grew both because of the compassion of the rescuers and a surge of inexperienced climbers who relied upon them.

Modern "pioneers" continued to find new challenges on the mountain. The East Buttress, a variant on the South Buttress and the Southeast Spur were climbed for the first time in the sixties. All of these hard new routes were completed with "style" and without accidents.

In July 1967, the largest tragedy on Denali took place. Since then, climbers have debated the real cause of the accident. One theory is that the National Park Service regulations forced two undersized groups to merge into one large one that had no real cohesiveness or leadership. Another theory suggests that a severe windstorm was the cause of the accident.

Nonetheless, the facts are hard to reconstruct because all six members of the second summit party were killed. After an unplanned bivouac at 19,500 feet, the climbers reached the summit. However, shortly afterward, they were caught in a windstorm and all perished. A seventh member of the group, who stayed behind at 17,900 feet, was also killed. (Five months before, three more experienced winter climbers coped with a similar windstorm and survived.) Fortunately, the team leader and three others had reached the summit the previous day and had then descended safely to 15,000 feet on the Harper Glacier. The seven bodies remained on the mountain as a grim reminder of an inexperienced team pitted against the ferocity of an unusual windstorm.

That same year, Boyd Everett, Jr. masterminded three simultaneous American ascents on the south side of the mountain:

the Cassin Ridge, the South Buttress and the hardest new route on the mountain, the American Direct south face.

While rappelling the Cassin Ridge at 15,000 feet (on Cassin's old fixed line), Bill Phillips fell 70 feet when the old rope broke. Although his Kelty pack and hard hat cushioned the fall, he hit his ankle but thought it was only a sprain. He descended the route under his own power and walked three miles' back to a landing site. X-rays later revealed that he had broken his ankle.

Meanwhile, the South Buttress party was hit by an avalanche at 11,500 feet. When an ice serac fell from 15,000 feet, two of the climbers were blown off their feet and into a crevasse more than 100 feet away. Two others were carried several hundred feet down the glacier. Except for a minor rib injury, all were unhurt and walked out 13 miles to the landing strip.

In an exemplary ascent of the hardest route on the mountain, the American Direct, all of the climbers emerged unscathed. There were no falls, no avalanches and no frostbite.

The 1960's marked the end of an era on Denali. A dozen books covering the pioneer period of the mountain's history were written. All of the major, logical new routes had been done. Climbing grew bolder and increasingly competitive, with higher standards of excellence. Quick, alpine-style climbs replaced fixed-rope tactics and technological advances made equipment warmer and lighter. Mountaineering became popular. Guide businesses started up. And the National Park Service began to require climbers to carry radios. As more and more people came, Denali lost its mystique. However, the mountain had not changed; as the number of climbers increased, so did the accidents.

Perhaps climbers were lulled into a false sense of security because of the possibility of rescue or by the belief that there was safety in numbers. Self-sufficiency was superseded by radios, helicopters and dependence on other climbers. All of these factors had an adverse effect, causing caution to be thrown to the winds; such behavior would have been foolhardy for the radioless, isolated pioneer climbers.

The 1970's brought a tremendous influx of a new breed of climbers and the boom began.

SUMMARY: THE SELF-SUFFICIENT PIONEERS

DATE	INCIDENT	NAME	ROUTE & ELEVATION OF INCIDENT
1932	CREVASSE FALL	CARPÉ KOVEN	MULDROW 9000
1953	FROSTBITE	HENNING	MULDROW 11000
1954	CLIMBING FALL	THAYER ARGUS	MULDROW 11000
1960	CLIMBING FALL	DAY SCHOENING	W BUTTRESS 18000
1960	HAPE	BADING	W BUTTRESS 16400
1960	FROSTBITE	*	W BUTTRESS 19500
1960	FROSTBITE	2 CANADIANS	W BUTTRESS 20000
1960	FROSTBITE	*	W BUTTRESS 19000
1960	SNOW BLINDNESS	2 CLIMBERS	W BUTTRESS *
1960	FROSTBITE	*	W BUTTRESS 19500
1961	FROSTBITE	CANALI	CASSIN 19000
1963	FROSTBITE	RGS CLIENT	W BUTTRESS 11000
WINTER 1967	CREVASSE FALL	BATKIN	W BUTTRESS 7000
WINTER 1967	FROSTBITE	JOHNSTON DAVIDSON	W BUTTRESS 18300
JULY 1967	HYPOTHERMIA	CLARK JANES LUCHTERHAND MCLAUGHLIN RUSSELL S TAYLOR W TAYLOR	MULDROW 17900–19500
AUGUST 1967	AVALANCHE	4 CLIMBERS	S BUTTRESS 11500
AUGUST 1967	CLIMBING FALL	PHILLIPS	CASSIN 15300

16

COMMENTS	HOW EVACUATED	RESULT
UNROPED	SLED	2 DEATHS
INADEQUATE LEATHER BOOTS	ON FOOT, HELICOPTER	*
SLIP ON DESCENT, UNFAMILIAR WITH KARSTENS RIDGE	LITTER, HELICOPTER	DEATH BROKEN HIP
RAPID ASCENT, SLIP ON DESCENT	HELICOPTER	BROKEN LEG CONCUSSION
LOWERED TO 14,200 FEET	LITTER, AIRPLANE	*
WINDY SUMMIT DAY	ON FOOT	FROSTBITE ON FINGERS
COLD SUMMIT DAY	ON FOOT	ALL TOES AMPUTATED
CRAMPON STRAPS TOO TIGHT	ON FOOT	FROSTBITE ON LARGE TOE
INADEQUATE AMBER SUNGLASSES	ON FOOT	TEMPORARY SNOWBLINDNESS
INADEQUATE BOOTS	ON FOOT	FROSTBITE ON FEET
ALPINE CLOTHING, STORMY SUMMIT DAY	ON FOOT	MILD FROSTBITE
BREAKING TRAIL WITHOUT SNOWSHOES	ON FOOT	FROSTBITE ON FEET
UNROPED	SLED	DEATH
WINDSTORM FORCED 6-DAY BIVOUAC	HELICOPTER (13150')	PARTIAL AMPUTATION 3 TOES 1 TOE AMPUTATED
WINDSTORM, INEXPERIENCE		7 DEATHS
SERAC AT 15000'	ON FOOT	1 MINOR RIB INJURY
RAPPELLING ON OLD FIXED ROPE	ON FOOT	BROKEN ANKLE

*INDICATES INFORMATION NOT AVAILABLE

C H A P T E R

High Altitude Pulmonary Edema

*Without the rapid descent
before the fluid buildup in my lungs
got worse, I would have been
yet another statistic on Denali.*

Jonathan Waterman

n June 24, 1976, I watched a Japanese climber lurch into the 14,300-foot West Buttress camp and collapse. Later that evening his friends came to us asking for help. Even ten yards away from the Japanese tent, you could hear the victim's labored breathing. His pulse was 130, then 140, and he lost consciousness. A few hours later, a helicopter landed and whisked the climber to the hospital; he made a rapid recovery with the descent.

Although climbing high too quickly can often bring on high altitude pulmonary edema (HAPE), it also has a lot to do with individual physiology. The unpredictable nature of HAPE dictates that anyone sleeping above 12,000 feet is a potential victim. Therefore, all climbers must alert themselves to the initial symptoms.

Judging by the experience of many climbers, Denali is higher than corresponding Himalayan or South American altitudes. Consequently, Denali mut be treated as a bigger mountain than most. For instance, the condition of climbers at 17,200-foot camps on Denali often deteriorates. But if these same climbers were at 17,000 feet in the Himalaya, the camp would allow for rest and recovery. Certainly one of the recurring causes of HAPE on Denali is climbing too quickly. Too often, climbers fly in from 300 feet above sea level in Talkeetna to the 7,000-foot glacier, but allow no acclimatization period for such a substantial altitude gain.

HAPE is a form of high-altitude illness that is dangerous largely because of its rapid onset. Because it isn't diagnosed in its early stages, HAPE often reaches life threatening proportions within hours. Initial symptoms include fatigue, breathlessness, an increased respiratory rate and a dry cough. The symptoms of acute mountain sickness (AMS, another form of high altitude illness that often precedes HAPE) include headache, insomnia, dehydration, nausea, lack of appetite, and swelling of hands, feet and face. Both HAPE and high altitude cerebral edema (HACE) involve abnormal fluid shifts to the lungs or brain.

After the evacuation of the Japanese climber, a guided Rainier Mountaineering, Inc. party came into camp. One of the clients had had trouble keeping up with the rest of the group. After a rest day at 14,300 feet, he too contracted HAPE; he was evacuated by helicopter. The group had taken five days to reach 14,300 feet—only a moderately fast pace. Perhaps, if the guides had allowed a rest day at 11,000 feet, the man would have acclimatized better. On Denali, the weakest member of a group always suffers when his shortcomings are overlooked so that the strongest members may achieve its goals.

Both of these experiences provided a sobering introduction to HAPE. As drowning in one's fluids seemed to be such a grisly fate, our group discussed the various means of preventing such an occurrence: drink four quarts of liquid a day, avoid strenuous

22

days with too much altitude gain, and descend immediately if headaches, nausea, AMS, or signs of HAPE were present.

Several days later, on July 2, a Genet guided party stopped at 16,200 feet because one of the clients was too tired to continue, despite climbing slowly and following the rules of acclimatization. The next night he developed HAPE and was given Lasix, a diuretic that drains fluids from the body.

Ray Genet carried him down to 14,300 feet where a doctor examined him. He then became unconscious; a frothy, bloody sputum issued from his mouth, while rales could be heard in his chest. (Rales indicate fluid in the lungs. Heard through a stethoscope, or with an ear to the victim's back, they sound like a lock of hair being rubbed between one's fingers.) His pulse climbed to 140 and his condition deteriorated rapidly. No helicopter could land in the stormy weather, and since there was no bottled oxygen in camp, within two hours of reaching 14,300 feet, he died.

It seemed wrong to see the 24-year-old wrapped in an American flag while 6,000 feet above, 80 people celebrated the Bicentennial. When I learned that the victim had contracted HAPE on a previous trip, the picture grew clearer. I continued to learn about HAPE from the mistakes of others, and six years later, would learn as a victim.

In 1978, Galen Rowell and Ned Gillette climbed from 10,000 feet to the summit (20,320 feet) within 24 hours. Their plan was to move faster than altitude illness could manifest itself. During the descent, however, Rowell made the mistake of sleeping at 17,200 feet, where he contracted HAPE. Fortunately, Gary Bocarde nursed the two climbers inside of his tent—hardly a self-sufficient speed climb. A rapid descent in the morning eliminated Rowell's symptoms.

Countless other world-class climbers "race," then "beat"

23

HAPE down the mountain. No doubt there have been many similar cases in which climbers were not even aware they had HAPE because they simply descended so quickly that the symptoms never became debilitating. But regardless of experience, many climbers are not capable of pulling off one-day ascents, and climbing too quickly for proper acclimatization is deadly.

In 1979, bad weather delayed the West German Mount McKinley Expedition. After flying to the 7,000-foot landing strip, they immediately began a rapid ascent despite an earlier warning from Park Rangers to climb slowly. Two days later, Georg Wudi developed HAPE and the party stamped out an S O S in the snow at 12,500 feet on the West Buttress. On July 1, pilot Jim Sharp saw the signal, landed at 14,300 feet and determined through a radio call that the Germans wanted a helicopter for Wudi. Sharp instructed them to move him down to 11,000 feet, which they did in two hours with help from another party. Sharp then landed his Cessna 185 and loaded Wudi on board. Sharp refused to take any gear or one of the healthy Germans who wanted a flight out.

Wudi had been cautioned against fast ascents. If the team had allowed more time for the climb, it is unlikely that he would have contracted HAPE. Furthermore, calling for an air evacuation at 12,500 feet is unnecessary—the Germans should have simply sledded the victim down several thousand feet until his condition improved.

The following year, another German team fell victim to their tight schedule. After sitting out a week of bad weather in Talkeetna, the team changed their plans from a quick climb of the Cassin to an even quicker climb of the West Buttress. On May 27, Konrad Schuhmann became sick at 14,300 feet. The next night he began to spit blood, so the group started to descend. When Schuhmann failed to improve after receiving a 20 mg injection of Lasix, they radioed for an evacuation.

That same night, helicopter pilot Jim Okonek picked up the semiconscious Schuhmann at 12,800 feet. Okonek thought Schuhmann was the sickest climber he had seen in years of helicopter evacuations. However, back down at 300 feet in the higher barometric pressure of Talkeetna, Schuhmann walked off the ship, declining further medical treatment.

In May 1981, three American speed climbers went from 7,000 feet to 14,300 feet in one day. They planned to acclimatize at 14,300 feet on the West Buttress, descend to the landing strip at 7,000 feet and then set a speed record to the summit. After the first night at 14,300 feet, one of the group began spitting up blood. All three then descended quickly before his condition became debilitating. (I saw him at 10,000 feet, moving slowly and staining the snow red.) The strongest climber did make a summit attempt from the landing strip but, after 12 hours, turned back at 17,200 feet because he felt sick.

As climbing to 14,000 feet in just one day is extremely fast, it could almost be expected that someone would get HAPE. The strongest climber felt that his mistake was in not spending more time acclimatizing at 14,300 feet prior to the summit attempt.

At the same time, a German team made a fast ascent of the West Buttress. They flew to 7,000 feet. During the night, Wolfgang Weinzierl suffered HAPE; knowing his limitations, however, (he had previously contracted HAPE in the Himalaya and in Peru), he descended at noon the next day. When he reached 14,300 feet, he was coughing and weak; on May 26, a Park Service patrol helped him down to 11,000 feet. As he continued down to the landing strip, his condition improved rapidly.

Weinzierl's immediate descent was exemplary. However, as

some individuals are more susceptible to HAPE than others, it is curious that Weinzierl chose to climb fast and risk HAPE after experiencing it twice before.

On the heels of Weinzierl's aborted speed climb, a five-man German group went from 7,000 feet, on May 27, to 16,000 feet on June 1. After their carry to 16,000 feet, one of the climbers, Karl Muck, became ill at 14,300 feet. On June 2, he had rales in both lungs; Lasix was given intramuscularly and some improvement was noted. An evacuation was then initiated. At 1:45 P.M., Muck and one healthy member of the party were brought out by helicopter. Although Muck's condition improved considerably on the descent, he was still disoriented when he arrived in Talkeetna.

This is another example of a situation where HAPE might have been prevented with early detection of symptoms and immediate descent to 11,000 feet.

In the October 1980 issue of *Alpinismus*, Peter Habeler wrote an article about his visit to the mountain in 1980. In it he says, "Again and again, Mount McKinley is underestimated by climbers whose arrogance borders on stupidity." He was concerned about the large number of European climbers who were getting into trouble on the mountain because of unrealistic expectations and improper attitudes. Although optimism and boldness may be virtues, when climbers overestimate their abilities and underestimate Denali, accidents can occur.

Because of the thinner atmosphere over the poles of the earth, the barometric pressures on the summit of Denali are equal to much higher elevations in the Himalaya. And Denali's extreme cold is not found until elevations above 25,000 feet in the Himalaya. Consequently, Denali has to be treated like a cold Himalayan peak.

There is almost always an explanation for why climbers

contract HAPE on Denali. Improper acclimatization is the primary cause, and can be prevented by gradual ascents, proper fluid intake and avoidance of unnecessary exertion. Some people are more prone to HAPE than others and previous victims often have recurrences. Sleeping pills are respiratory depressants—a quick invitation to HAPE. And common bronchitis or pneumonia can also predispose one to HAPE.

Another factor contributing to HAPE is carbon monoxide poisoning from cooking in sealed tents, snow caves or igloos. In July 1974, a climber at 18,200 feet became ill from carbon monoxide poisoning which led to HAPE. He was dragged to 15,000 feet, where he received an oxygen air drop, and eventually, a helicopter evacuation. As in many cases of altitude sickness on Denali, oxygen can temporarily alleviate the problem, but when the supply runs out, the victim's condition will continue to deteriorate until death. Immediate descent is the only sure treatment.

Some climbers use Diamox to acclimatize more quickly. This respiratory stimulant is best used as a sleep aid for persons who have experienced headaches, insomnia, lack of appetite, nausea or lassitude (symptoms of AMS), despite having followed proper acclimatization techniques. It has never been shown to prevent HAPE, and its side effects—inability to taste beer, frequent urination, tingling in fingers and toes—are undesirable.

Most cases of HAPE occur during the ascent of Denali. It is the most common illness on the mountain and has led to at least three deaths, while dozens of victims have needed helicopter evacuations. Since 1982, Peter Hackett has treated dozens of climbers for HAPE at the 14,300-foot camp by putting them on oxygen overnight, thus allowing them to walk down safely in the morning. But perhaps twice that many people have walked down under their own power before symptoms immobilized them.

A body on the West Rib. *RAY GENET*

Dr. Ralph Bovard examining HAPE victim at the 14,300-foot medical camp. *JONATHAN WATERMAN*

Relying upon the medical camp for oxygen treatment, rather than walking down immediately, would be a deadly gamble.

Although prevention is the best cure, immediate descent is the only reliable treatment. There is nothing to be gained by waiting for helicopters that can be delayed by weather and mechanical breakdowns. Altitude, cold and high winds will only accelerate the chances of death, whereas rapid descent can save the life of a HAPE victim, as well as prevent a pilot from risking his life.

In May 1980, Mark Cupps, a client in a Fantasy Ridge group led by Michael Covington, collapsed with HAPE at 19,850 feet on the South Buttress while the group was making their second carry to the summit. Covington alerted a pilot, but was told that a helicopter evacuation was not possible at that altitude. Covington immediately started to move Cupps to a lower altitude, while the pilot tried to find a helicopter to meet them at 16,000 feet on the South Buttress. Five hours later, at 16,000 feet, Cupps' condition improved, but he still wanted to be evacuated. However, darkness prevented an Army helicopter from landing on the mountain that night.

The next morning, the helicopter broke down in Talkeetna, which meant a six-hour delay in the evacuation. Because of increasing clouds and poor visibility, Covington decided that descent was the best option, despite Cupps' insistence that he be rescued. As waiting for a helicopter was too risky, they descended and the rescue was called off. After reaching the glacier, Cupps' condition improved dramatically.

Covington's dynamic reaction to a HAPE victim should serve as an example for other climbers on the mountain. He initiated an immediate descent on his own rather than gambling on an unreliable helicopter evacuation. There have been instances where victims who waited for helicopters, instead of descending immediately, lapsed into unconsciousness. Descent is always the most proctical treatment for HAPE.

In March 1982, I learned about HAPE the hard way while trying to complete a winter climb of the Cassin Ridge. Two weeks earlier, I had contracted bronchitis. The cough went away on the glacier, and so I naively disregarded my potential for HAPE—certainly I had been to high altitude on a half dozen other trips and had never contracted it.

At 16,000 feet, I took a sleeping pill in order to be fully rested for the next day of climbing. Furthermore, our fear of a winter storm made us climb quickly, which gave my two partners and I headaches. After the sleeping pill, I was dizzy and had trouble breathing; Mike Young and Roger Mear had to wait for me, and were forced to bivouac at 19,600 feet because I was moving so slowly. The next morning I woke up in the midst of a drowning nightmare: I had fluid in my lungs and could barely breathe. When I stood up outside the tent, I had trouble keeping my balance. Crawling and stumbling to the summit ridge 500 feet above was the hardest act of my life.

Walking down the West Buttress, I could take only three steps before I had to rest and fight for ten more breaths. Although there was no blood or sputum, I coughed constantly. My companions disappeared down the route, and I fought to pull enough of the 50-degrees-below-zero air into my lungs. I felt overwhelmed by the effort, constantly tempted to lie down and sleep—then die. Even going downhill seemed unachievable.

Finally, at darkness I caught up to Young and Mear at 17,000 feet. I coughed all night. In the morning they dressed me. As I struggled down to 14,300 feet in the face of a coming storm, I felt as if there were a clamp on my bronchial tubes. Yet one night in the thicker air at 14,300 feet allowed me to recover from this moderate-to-severe HAPE. Another night up higher and I wouldn't have been able to walk.

Clearly, the bronchitis and sleeping pill predisposed me to HAPE. As is the case with many HAPE victims, the stress of the climb precluded proper acclimatization. Without the rapid descent, I would have become yet another statistic.

A year later, I rescued a victim who had made some of the same mistakes. In April 1983, three Germans rushed up to the 14,300-foot camp on the West Buttress in three days, despite feeling ill halfway up. Manfred Kessler's pulse climbed to 115, and although a doctor at the medical camp could not detect rales, he recommended immediate descent.

On April 29, Kessler went down to 12,900 feet. He had a headache, lack of balance, shortness of breath and coughed up pink, frothy sputum. Kessler took a sleeping pill and rested briefly, but his pulse climbed higher and he could no longer walk. I alerted helicopter pilot Chris Soloy, who flew to Talkeetna immediately.

We left for the mountain that afternoon. An hour later, while Soloy balanced his helicopter skid on the lip of the bergschrund at 12,900 feet, I jumped out and lifted Kessler into the tiny ship, then held a demand oxygen mask over his face. By the time we arrived back in Talkeetna, Kessler was lightheaded, but walked out of the ship unassisted.

Obviously, Kessler and his party climbed too quickly for proper acclimatization. Kessler shouldn't have taken a sleeping pill, and had he descended below 12,900 feet, in several days his condition might have improved enough to negate the helicopter, or to continue his climb.

Three months later, on July 25, Liao Kun-Shan and Sun Tz-Chuan gave up on the summit and turned around at 19,500 feet on the West Buttress with altitude illness. They were unroped and consequently, when Liao fell at 18,500 feet, he slid for nearly 300 feet and bruised his ribs. Nonetheless, the pair arrived back at 17,200 feet just before midnight.

They rested the next day, but Liao complained of chest pain where he jarred his ribs, breathing difficulties, weakness and an inability to eat or drink. Although they were with seven other Taiwanese, the team felt they lacked the experience to accompany Liao down.

The next day Liao had a dry cough and could barely walk—the Taiwanese radioed for a helicopter. Ranger Scott Gill and pilot Ron Smith, of ERA Helicopters, flew to the site; after many passes in the cloudy weather, Smith set the ship down near the Taiwanese camp while Gill jumped out and dragged Liao in. The victim was given oxygen, and as is often the case, he recovered dramatically by the time they landed in Talkeetna.

Had the relatively inexperienced summit climbers used a rope like most beginners, Liao probably wouldn't have fallen as far and injured himself. An immediate descent from the 17,200-foot camp would have been ideal, particularly with such beautiful weather and a team as large as theirs to assist Liao. Clearly the word has gotten out on Denali that a helicopter is much less work than a ground evacuation. Climbers such as these will someday be forced to learn self-sufficiency, but, unfortunately, not until after a helicopter crashes and rescuers become victims.

It is worth noting that, in 1984, my partner Karl Klassen—who worked at a ski area in Canada all winter at 9,000 feet—contracted mild AMS at 8,900 feet on the West Buttress route. Klassen felt better the next day, and since we were not at high altitude, insisted that we move to 10,000 feet. That night, Klassen began vomiting, had a severe headache, a temperature of 101 degrees and a bad cough. HAPE seemed so unlikely that even Dr. John Diaz diagnosed pneumonia.

33

In the morning, Klassen could barely stand up. We had waited long enough: Joe Kanetsky helped me sled Klassen down to 8,000 feet. Since Klassen was still incoherent and in and out of consciousness, I was concerned that sledding him another 1,000 feet lower to the landing strip would not help his condition. I immediately radioed Doug Geeting, who landed at 8,000 feet and flew Klassen out to Talkeetna.

Although his condition improved immediately, Klassen could not remember anything about his evacuation. At the Humana Hospital in Anchorage, he was diagnosed with severe HAPE; he was groggy for weeks. It is probable that if we had taken a rest day at 8,900 feet, Klassen's condition would have improved. Nonetheless, this remains the only recorded incident of HAPE below 10,000 feet; it will happen again.

In 1985, during a five-day stretch of good weather on the mountain, four climbers from different teams contracted HAPE. The weather had been continuously bad prior to this period, so climbers jockeyed to get to the summit as quickly as possible. An American climbed from the landing strip to 17,200 feet in six days; while a German, a Frenchman, and a Japanese each took four days to get to the 14,300-foot camp from the landing strip. All were given various advice, oxygen or Diamox at the medical camp before descending.

Prior to the medical camp's presence, these victims' conditions might have deteriorated until either death or a helicopter took them away. Although 85 percent of the traffic on Denali goes up the West Buttress, virtually all serious cases of HAPE occur there. The implications are that West Buttress climbers are generally inexperienced and ill prepared, while climbers tackling more remote and difficult routes are more self-sufficient and take the proper preventative measures against HAPE, when it does occur, they perform their own quiet evacuations.

In this same stretch of good weather, Yoshikatsu Sumimoto (37) and his four companions took a leisurely week to reach 12,800 feet (more than sufficient time to acclimatize). On the evening of May 1, Sumimoto had trouble breathing and his lungs gurgled. In the morning he coughed bloody sputum and standing up was difficult. His party took him down to 11,000 feet, where Rick Maschek recommended they continue to an igloo at 9,000 feet.

Later that evening, Maschek brought down a radio, a bottle of oxygen, and some Diamox, but found that the Japanese had not descended below 11,000 feet, while Sumimoto was left unattended in a tent by himself. He had a pulse of 120, respirations of 28 and a temperature of 101 degrees (typical in HAPE victims). Maschek administered 500 mg of Diamox, put Sumimoto on a low flow of oxygen and then badgered the Japanese into giving fluids and carefully monitoring their sick companion.

By the morning of May 3, Sumimoto's pulse had dropped below 100 and he was able to sit up. Later that day the team skied out to base camp.

The oxygen may well have saved Sumimoto's life. However, a descent of at least 3,000 feet would have helped greatly, as well as a bit more dynamism and compassion from the man's teammates.

This peculiar Japanese lack of concern and compassion for an ailing teammate was re-enacted on May 25, 1987. On that day, Sachikie Takada descended to 14,300 feet from 17,200 feet with her two companions because the weather was bad and she was ill.

Two days later, some French climbers noticed Takada's weakness, and moved her by sled to the nearby medical camp. She was diagnosed with HAPE, but after 24 hours of oxygen and

35

Diamox, she still could not walk. Rob Roach organized a ground team that sledded her down to 11,000 feet; her partners were very unhelpful during the evacuation. Once she reached base camp and was flown to Talkeetna, she recovered.

What a terrible irony it would have been if the French climbers had not noticed Takada, and she had died next to her uncaring partners' tent, a camp of 70 climbers and an elaborate medical facility.

The medical camp would save yet another life on June 8, 1990. The day before, Craig Scott, a triathlete and a Rainier Mountaineering, Inc. client, had trouble sleeping and breathing. However, he did not tell his guides until he needed help walking late the next morning. At the medical camp, he was diagnosed with severe HAPE and given oxygen at a high flow for four hours. That night, breathing from an oxygen bottle, he walked down to 8,000 feet, where his condition improved rapidly.

Certainly, Scott should have told the guides about his difficulties as soon as they arose. Although Scott was a trained athlete, nothing short of an oxygen bottle or immediate descent can overcome HAPE. It is interesting to note that many HAPE victims in recent years have simply descended 3,000 feet, reacclimatized, and then reached the summit a week or two later.

One can only guess how many climbers might have died from HAPE if the medical camp had not been set up (for independent research, not to rescue climbers) at 14,300 feet in 1982. Now too many climbers rely upon the oxygen and expertise of the doctors. This not only reduces Denali's difficulty, but reflects poorly upon the esthetics of those who come each year to climb North America's highest peak.

Recommendations? Proceed as if the medical camp doesn't

exist. Listen to your body and climb conservatively. Avoid sleeping pills, salty food, cooking in sealed tents, caves or igloos. Cover your mouth with a thin balaclava to minimize loss of heat and moisture from the lungs, and approach HAPE as if it were yet another objective danger, encountered with all the frequency of avalanches. Study it, fear it, think preventatively.

If HAPE does strike someone in your party, descend immediately, minimize any exertion by the victim, and be prepared to evacuate him yourselves, with no oxygen, medical camp, or helicopters.

SUMMARY: HIGH ALTITUDE PULMONARY EDEMA

DATE	NAME	ROUTE & ELEVATION OF INCIDENT	COMMENTS
7/6/74	HEGGERNESS	W BUTTRESS 18300	CARBON MONOXIDE POISONING
6/21/76	RAINIER MOUNTAINEERING	W BUTTRESS 14300	COULDN'T KEEP PACE, TOO FAST
6/24/76	WAKABAYASHI (JAPAN)	W BUTTRESS 14300	TOO FAST
7/1/76	GULEKE (GENET-PORZAK)	W BUTTRESS 16200	PREVIOUS HAPE
1978	ROWELL	W BUTTRESS 17200	TOO FAST
7/1/79	WUDI	W BUTTRESS 12500	TOO FAST
5/1/80	CUPPS (FANTASY RIDGE)	S BUTTRESS 19850	
6/1/80	SCHUHMANN	W BUTTRESS 14300	TOO FAST
5/25/81	SPEED CLIMBERS USA	W BUTTRESS 14300	TOO FAST
5/26/81	WEINZIERL	W BUTTRESS 17200	PREVIOUS HAPE, TOO FAST
6/2/81	MUCK	W BUTTRESS 14300	TOO FAST
3/6/82	WATERMAN	CASSIN 19600	BRONCHITIS PREDIS- POSED, SLEEPING PILL
4/29/83	KESSLER	W BUTTRESS 12900	TOO FAST, SLEEPING PILL
7/25/83	LIAO KUN-SHAN	W BUTTRESS 17200	UNROPED, NO ATTEMPT TO EVACUATE
5/1/85	YOSHIKATSU SUMIMOTO	W BUTTRESS 12800	INABILITY TO DESCEND
5/25/87	SACHIKIE TAKADA	W BUTTRESS 14300	UNCONCERNED PARTNERS
6/8/90	CRAIG SCOTT	W BUTTRESS 14300	WAITED TOO LONG TO REPORT

38

HOW EVACUATED	RESULT	RESCUED BY	GOVERNMENT COST
HELICOPTER	RECOVERED	ARMY	$3000
HELICOPTER	RECOVERED	*	$3385.50
HELICOPTER	RECOVERED	WOODS AIR SERVICE	$1740.39
HELICOPTER	DEATH	WOODS AIR SERVICE	*
ON FOOT	RECOVERED		NONE
HELICOPTER	RECOVERED	JIM SHARP	*(WUDI PAID)
ON FOOT	RECOVERED	ARMY	*
HELICOPTER	RECOVERED	AKLAND HELICOP-TER SERVICE	$849.06
ON FOOT	RECOVERED		NONE
ON FOOT	RECOVERED		NONE
HELICOPTER	RECOVERED	ALASKA HELICOPTERS	$2013.12 (MUCK PAID)
ON FOOT	RECOVERED		NONE
HELICOPTER	RECOVERED	SOLOY HELICOPTERS, NPS	$1767
HELICOPTER	RECOVERED	ERA HELICOPTERS, NPS	$4678
SELF	RECOVERED	RICK MASCHEK	NONE
SLED	RECOVERED	FRENCH, AMERICANS, ROB ROACH	NONE
WALKED DOWN	RECOVERED	SELF	NONE

*INDICATES INFORMATION NOT AVAILABLE

CHAPTER THREE

High Altitude Cerebral Edema

Ten climbers were killed
in the Park in 1980; Simon and I
were lucky to have survived

Bob Kandiko in
THE AMERICAN ALPINE JOURNAL 1981

Imagine cerebral edema: fluid collects inside the brain causing constant headaches, then comes loss of balance; as the pressure continues building inside the skull, victims have also experienced apathy, hallucinations, seizures, failure of motor function, unconsciousness and, without descent, death. Two climbers have died on Denali from high altitude cerebral edema (HACE) and dozens have had close calls.

The symptoms of HACE are headaches, vomiting, lassitude, reduced urine output and, most often, loss of balance or ataxia. This loss of balance is what differentiates HACE from high altitude pulmonary edema (HAPE), although some of the same symptoms may be present in both. Also, victims of severe HAPE will often develop HACE. To check for ataxia, a loss of balance caused by a lack of oxygen in the cerebellum, one should walk on a straight line drawn in the snow, heel to toe. If the victim can't keep his balance, immediate descent is indicated. As in HAPE, oxygen will be useful; but if it is not available in adequate quantities, descent is the only sure cure. The drug Decadron (Dexamethasone) can also be useful, but is no substitute for descent. Although it is not always possible to prevent HACE, careful monitoring of all party members can help to avoid needless loss of life and costly rescues.

On June 9, 1978, Bruce Hickson and Tom Crouch, who were with an Air Force Pararescue climbing team, were both stricken with altitude sickness at Denali Pass. Hickson had HACE and Crouch had acute mountain sickness (AMS). (Hickson had climbed Denali the previous year without experiencing any serious altitude problems.) The next day they were evacuated by an Army helicopter. The two climbers had been taking Diamox to prevent altitude sickness, but had stopped taking it during the second half of their trip when their supply ran out; this may have predisposed them to altitude sickness.

Five days later, on June 15, a guided team reached 14,300 feet on the West Buttress, Charles Prentice, a client, complained of a headache for the next three days, but seemed to perform as well as the rest of the group while carrying loads to 16,200 feet. On the fourth day, Prentice lost his sleeping bag; he then borrowed a bivouac sack. When the group reached 17,200 feet, Prentice had a bad headache. Twenty-four hours later, the weather had deteriorated and Prentice's headache was severe. The guide decided to take him down in the morning. However, during the night, the wind picked up, and the group was forced to abandon their tents and move into igloos for the next two days.

Prentice's condition deteriorated. He became incoherent, could walk only with difficulty, and ate and drank very little; his headaches were severe and painful. He was given an hour of oxygen that was left over from a previous rescue. The guide remained with Prentice at 17,200 feet; the rest of the group

44

descended to 14,300 feet because the guide decided they were too weak to evacuate Prentice. The climbers tried to organize a ground rescue team but failed; they then called the National Park Service for a helicopter evacuation.

During the next two days, Prentice was unconscious at times. On the third day, a helicopter landed and evacuated both the guide and Prentice from 17,200 feet. As Prentice had slept apart from the rest of the group, the guide may not have been aware of his condition. The fate of clients who climb on Denali rests entirely on their guide's leadership and judgment. Ideally, because of his headaches, Prentice's condition should have been monitored more carefully, and he should have been escorted down immediately. The guide was issued a citation by the National Park Service because he had not gotten a business permit or registered as a guide.

The following year, 1979, four Germans made the classic mistake in high-altitude adaptation when they climbed from the 7,000-foot landing strip to the 16,400-foot West Buttress camp in three days. On the fourth day, they left for the summit. Valentin Demmel, Jr. and Guenter Kroh stopped at Denali Pass to camp, while Valentin Demmel, Sr. and Andreas Kahnt continued to the summit. Immediately after they reached the summit, Kahnt became seriously ill with HACE; Demmel had to carry him most of the way down. They took ten hours to return to Denali Pass.

Meanwhile, Kroh and Demmel Jr. had become alarmed at their partners' prolonged absence. Kroh, who was suffering from altitude sickness, descended to 17,200 feet and radioed the National Park Service requesting an evacuation.

That same day Kroh was evacuated by airplane from 14,300 feet, while Kahnt and Demmel Jr. were picked up by helicopter from Denali Pass. Demmel recovered quickly. Both Kahnt and Kroh were treated for frostbite.

The ramifications of a fast ascent are obvious. One group who saw the Germans on their summit day tried to talk them out of the attempt because they appeared to be ill prepared. Splitting up the team on a summit day is a frequent prelude to accidents on Denali. When a team is divided, it usually becomes weaker, as smaller groups are less capable of self-evacuation should an accident occur.

Two weeks later, despite maintaining an average pace up the West Buttress, one member of the Montana Denali Expedition suffered from HACE. After a rest day at 17,200 feet, James Krudener and his partner started for the summit. Krudener returned an hour later complaining of dizziness and went to sleep. During the night, his condition worsened and he developed bad headaches. The next day, he seemed a little better and could walk. On the descent, however, he was disoriented and his condition deteriorated again. At 16,000 feet, he had to be partly lowered down the fixed lines.

A doctor with Ray Genet's party treated Krudener at the 14,300-foot camp. Although he gave Krudener fluids, his condition did not improve; the next morning he became incoherent and could not drink. The doctor suspected HACE and dehydration. He gave Krudener some oxygen and Lasix. That morning, Krudener had a seizure and, at one point, stopped breathing.

Cliff Hudson was notified in the afternoon and, shortly afterwards, landed his plane at 14,300 feet and evacuated Krudener to the hospital in Anchorage. That night the hospital reported that Krudener was in critical but stable condition.

Unless Krudener had not been eating and drinking properly, he is an example of a climber who contracts HACE despite proper preventive maintenance. Had Krudener remained another day at 17,200 feet, it is unlikely that he would have survived.

It is probable that a third climber suffered from HACE in June 1979. However, due to the language barrier imposed during an interview with the Japanese climbers, the information received was limited. A four-man Japanese expedition fixed ropes from 12,000 to 16,000 feet, up 50 pitches of rock, on a new Southwest Face route. They placed no camps on the face and, on June 27, made a 16-hour, continuous summit bid from 12,000 feet! Their high point was 16,500 feet, where all four members contracted AMS. In the afternoon, Mitsuyasu Hamatani became very sick, so the leader radioed that he "would die tonight" if he were not rescued.

A day later, Hamatani was evacuated from the face in an unprecedented high-altitude winching operation. The three other climbers traversed down to the West Rib route. Hamatani was flown to Providence Hospital in Anchorage and released several hours later in "good condition." It is possible that Hamatani's HACE was overlooked at the hospital, since edema victims often recover very rapidly upon descent. Although the analysis in the 1980 *Accidents in North American Mountaineering* reported that there was "no apparent need for rescue," the team, which had been to high altitude in the Himalaya, told a Japanese interpreter in Anchorage that Hamatani had HACE. (This is not difficult for experienced altitude climbers to diagnose.)

The Japanese team's climbing style may have been a bit presumptuous for Denali. A summit bid, with one intermediate camp between 12,000 and 20,000 feet, is an unlikely proposition. All of the team had altitude sickness, which seems to verify the fact that they had climbed too fast in 16 hours. As has been the case with many other climbers in a jam on Denali,

47

safety outweighed esthetics during their retreat, and nearly 4,000 feet of fixed line remained to litter the route.

A year later, in 1980, the prophetically self-named "Too Loose" expedition chose to do the Southwest Face in an esthetically impeccable style: fast and light, with no fixed ropes, which also proved their undoing. Jack Roberts and Simon McCartney ran out of food at 16,000 feet but, with the technical difficulties behind them, they decided to go for the top. They eventually traversed to the Cassin route and two days later, at 19,200 feet, McCartney contracted HACE. When two other climbers on the Cassin, Mike Helms and Bob Kandiko, discovered them, they had been without food or water for four days. This probably predisposed McCartney to altitude sickness and Roberts to frostbite.

An example of how difficult a rescue on technical terrain can be is well defined in Bob Kandiko's account from the 1981 *American Alpine Journal:*

> Try to imagine the scene: Four climbers, one who is semi-conscious, try to sort out what is left of their brains in an attempt to save each others' lives. Jack, who has assisted in big-wall rescues in Yosemite, believes a winch and cable can be dropped on the crest above. Simon can be hauled up the south face and then an air evacuation can transport him off the mountain. Mike, who is trained in mountain rescue, believes a party from the West Buttress can trudge over the summit and carry Simon over and down the tourist route. Simon mutters something about a helicopter plucking us directly off the ridge. I sit totally befuddled while dishing out the soup. So much for rational thought at 19,500 feet.
>
> A decision is made: Mike, who is familiar with the West Buttress from previous trips, will take frostbitten Jack over while I stay to nurse Simon. Once they reach a group with a

radio (we had no radio because it saved weight), a rescue can be coordinated. Surely this will take just a couple of days. After all, this is Mount McKinley where rescues are commonplace!

From this point (called Day 1) Mike's and my stories are distinctly separate but ultimately integrated as we struggle to get off the mountain. Without radios we have no knowledge of the decisions being made on the opposite side of McKinley. The ensuing account reveals the astonishing sequence of events that bring us down Mount McKinley.

Day 1: Simon spends a fitful day passing in and out of consciousness. I give him a cup of soup or tea every hour. As night approaches I curl up next to him to transfer body heat.

Mike and Jack summit in four hours and trudge down to Denali Pass where they find a Mountain Trip expedition camped. Due to harsh atmospheric conditions, radio contact is impossible from Denali Pass.

Day 2: Simon's temperature returns to normal as the soup is finished and the remaining tea is kicked over; we have no food left. An irritating groin rash causes Simon severe pain until a skin ointment is salvaged from the first-aid kit.

Mike and Jack are tent-bound due to high winds and poor visibility. Still no radio contact about Simon's condition has reached the Park Service.

Day 3: Simon and I decide to try for the summit crest to save ourselves. As we begin to pack, two starved and frostbitten Scottish climbers appear on their way to the summit. They are too exhausted and ill to lend assistance but their footsteps should aid in our attempt. An hour later Simon and I rope up and begin our ascent. In two hours we travel barely a quarter mile as Simon cannot maintain his balance and is too weak to stand. We retrace our steps and erect the tent. Hot water is served for dinner.

Mike and Jack descend to 17,200 feet and locate a radio. The message detailing Simon's condition is received by Frances Randall at Kahiltna airstrip at three P.M. The Mountain Trip expedition from Denali Pass leaves for the summit.

Day 4: Simon and I have been awake most of the night using the stove to heat ourselves. It is crucial that we descend. We repack the gear, swallow Dexedrines for breakfast, and begin the arduous descent of the Cassin Ridge. Simon glissades on his seat while I belay, then I walk down. The clouds move in as a plane engine is heard. In poor visibility the plane signals it has seen us as we struggle onto a snow arête at 18,300 feet. We believe a rescue by helicopter now has been initiated. I stamp out the word "rescue" in the snow and we set up the tent and begin another wait. . . .

Day 5: No rescue has arrived. This is my fourth day without food while Simon has had one meal in the last six days. Our feeling of isolation and subsequent depression are acute. Tomorrow we will continue down. We resort to "toothpaste soup" in hopes of retarding our dehydration. This *soup de jour* causes indigestion but serves as an excellent decongestant. . . .

On a fly-by Doug Geeting and Park Ranger [Roger Robinson] spotted Simon and me descending the Cassin Ridge. We appeared tired but capable of moving so no rescue has been organized. Our crucial food shortage was obviously not emphasized through radio contact.

Day 6: Simon and I get motivated by Dexedrines and stumble down to an old campsite at 17,000 feet. The last gallon of fuel is retrieved from the cache and used tea bags are extricated from the snow. Above the campsite two coils of climbing rope are miraculously discovered. These will be used in rappelling the upper rock band. The diluted tea created optimism on my fifth day without food.

Heavy snows and high winds prevent a rescue attempt from the West Buttress.

Day 7: Barely able to stand, Simon and I begin the rappels. Frustration results in tears as we struggle to find anchors in the rock. Halfway through the rockband we spot four climbers erecting a tent on the slope below. As luck would have it, the ropes get caught on the next rappel. We are too weak to jumar up to unhook the snag and so we continue down with only one rope. Six hours after leaving 17,000 feet we collapse into the climbers' arms. . . .

Day 8: In the company of the four Pennsylvania climbers, Simon and I rappel the lower rockband just in time to catch a Japanese party which is also retreating after an unsuccessful attempt on the Cassin. They have a radio and call Frances Randall indicating that we are alive but in desperate need of food. She contacts the park rangers who are about to leave Talkeetna to evacuate Wolfgang. Within an hour a food-drop is made on the hanging glacier at 14,300 feet and Wolfgang is on his way to Anchorage. Jack is flown out from the glacier by Geeting and is taken to Anchorage hospital for frostbite treatment.

Day 9: Simon and I descend the ice arête with the inexperienced and frightened Pennsylvanians who use pitons for brake bars and want to rappel the arête instead of moving along the new fixed line. We finally reach the glacier at the base of the Japanese Couloir. Simon has contracted severe trench foot and can barely walk.

Day 10: In white-out conditions Simon and I follow faint footsteps down the Northeast Fork. In the upper icefall we encounter a steep icy slope. I start down on belay only to slip and begin somersaulting. Simon is pulled off his stance. Incredibly I post-hole a leg which stops my fall. The rope jerks tight as Simon freefalls 50 feet into a crevasse. Now he is completely incapacitated with a broken wrist and a severe concussion. Fortunately the trailing Japanese party and a Minneapolis group camped below extricate Simon from the lower lip of the crevasse. Simon is carried to their camp where another radio message is made.

Day 11: The Minneapolis group generously shares its food with us as the clouds move in to prevent the authorized helicopter rescue.

Day 12: After two days of waiting at the junction of the Northeast Fork, Ranger Dave Buchanan convinces two Swiss mountain guides to accompany him up the glacier to haul Simon down in a toboggan. At 8:30 P.M. Simon is enclosed in a bivy sac, tied onto the rescue sled, and the long trip to the airstrip is started. With the help of 20 climbers from Kahiltna airstrip, Simon reaches the southeast fork at four A.M. When the clouds finally part at eleven A.M., Geeting zips in and flies Simon and two frostbite victims directly to Anchorage.

Although Roberts' frostbite was due to a lack of food and water, it is difficult to attribute McCartney's HACE to any one mistake in particular. Certainly he contracted immersion (trench) foot because he never took off his boots during the climb.

Their rescue illustrates the slim chances of a helicopter evacuation from a route like the Cassin that lacks landing sites, despite some of the more recent helicopter winching operations on this side of the mountain. Sick climbers on technical routes, particularly without radios, must be prepared to descend immediately before altitude compounds the problem.

John Roskelley, one of the most accomplished American climbers in the Himalaya, fell victim to a cerebral vascular spasm (cortical blindness) in 1981 while attempting a quick ascent of the Cassin Ridge. Roskelley and his partner had climbed to 18,000 feet in three days. A carbon dioxide imbalance causes this seldom diagnosed problem which rendered

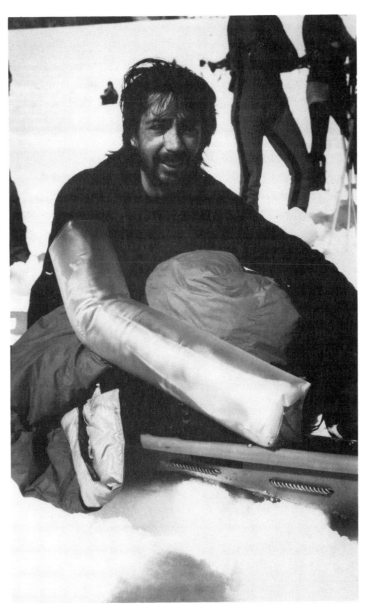

Simon McCartney at the landing strip after his rescue from the Cassin Ridge. *DAVE BUCHANAN*

Roskelley periodically blind. (Dr. Peter Hackett has now examined over a dozen victims on Denali who have temporarily lost their vision.) Fortunately, they retreated immediately. The summit was close but descent was the only real cure—although breathing into a bag to allow carbon dioxide to build up might have helped. They rappelled back down the Cassin Ridge, utilizing numerous pieces of fixed protection. Roskelley felt that he had underestimated Denali.

In 1986, the first of four Korean debacles began on the Cassin Ridge. On June 16, Lee Jong Kwan and Chung Seoung Kwon camped at 19,700 feet after a very fast four days of climbing. British climbers Mo Antoine, Joe Brown, J.H. Stokes, and Trevor Pilling passed by and thought it strange that the Koreans should camp so close to the summit. Lee had a severe headache and became ataxic. Eventually, the pair realized they were too weak to go up and lacked a second rope to rappel with; they assumed a helicopter would simply pluck them off. So, on June 19, they began broadcasting a very garbled S O S on their radio. Because of the language barrier, no one understood they needed a rescue until the next day.

Down in Talkeetna, the four British climbers volunteered to be helicoptered to 17,200 feet on the West Buttress, then walk up and perform the rescue, since they were acclimatized and knew the Koreans' location. But at 4:00 A.M. on June 21, the British were so terribly hungover that they couldn't get out of bed; an hour and a half was lost recruiting other rescuers. By the time the five-man rescue team was airborne, the weather closed in at 17,200 feet, so pilot Ron Smith of ERA Helicopters had to drop the team off at 14,300 feet on the West Buttress.

Only one of the five, Vern Tejas, was able to continue above 18,200 feet. The rescue operation involved over two dozen people, perhaps the biggest effort since the Day rescue of 1960.

By 8:00 P.M., Tejas reached the summit ridge and rappelled down his 600-foot rope to the Koreans. He gave Lee 10 mg of Decadron, some food and water, then helped Lee climb back to the summit ridge. Once on top, Lee fell into a coma. Fortunately, Wolfgang Wippler, another member of the rescue team arrived, and the two of them began dragging Lee down the West Buttress route in a small plastic sled; Chung stumbled along in the rear.

After another day of intense effort, Lee was dragged to 17,200 feet and picked up in the early morning of June 23. In Talkeetna, he recovered immediately. Without the intensive and selfless efforts of Tejas, Wippler, and many others, Lee would surely have died. Certainly, the British indiscretion could have cost Lee his life, as well as that of several rescuers who lost valuable time by not being dropped off at 17,200 feet.

In the final analysis, the Koreans climbed too quickly. They were ill advised not only in choosing to camp at 19,700 feet, but in thinking that a rest day at that altitude would allow them to recover. They should have gone over the summit or retreated entirely.

An important technique that gained popularity during the eighties—for those wishing to prevent altitude sickness during fast, alpine-style ascents—is to climb up to 17,200 feet on the West Buttress to acclimatize and leave a food cache before attempting a fast climb of another route. Rapid, unacclimatized ascents have few advantages when one considers how many climbers have contracted high-altitude sickness.

In 1988, Lee returned to the Cassin Ridge, unacclimatized again and little the wiser after his first lucky escape. First though, comes the story of his countryman Sung Hyun Baek who began soloing the Cassin Ridge. Baek climbed very quickly and caught up to Lee and his companion at 18,200 feet, but could no longer walk, probably because of AMS and exhaustion. None of the climbers had a rope to descend with, so they called for a rescue. Since the rangers have to assume that someone is in serious trouble when a rescue is called for, Baek was winched off by an army Chinook helicopter the next day—the highest winching operation ever performed in North America. Afterward, examination revealed that he was only suffering from minor frostbite on two fingers.

The day after the Baek's winching, Lee's companion Hyun Young Chung suffered a very serious stroke and HACE. Chung could not move his legs. So seven days later, the pair were both winched by another Chinook helicopter. This time, however, the evacuation saved Chung's life. During the winching, while clipped into his harness by a cable and suspended below a rotor wash with a 100-mph wind chill, Chung froze his fingers because he was not wearing gloves.

Again, both rescues could have been avoided had the Koreans acclimatized on the West Buttress prior to their climb. A fourth rescue involving Korean climbers would also take place on the Cassin Ridge (see Frostbite chapter).

Eight years earlier, on the other side of the mountain, an inexplicable incident occurred. On June 12, 1980, Czechoslovakians Jan Mikeska, Dan Navratil and Jan Matus left from 16,100 feet on the Harper Glacier for the summit. Their companion, Jiri Novotny, was not feeling well and stayed in camp. At 19,300 feet, the climbers passed the bodies of two Germans who had sat down and died in a storm two weeks before; only Mikeska remembered seeing them.

Navratil and Matus were extremely weak and felt that they could not continue to the top. They decided that Mikeska should continue alone, and that Matus and Navratil would descend and wait for him at Denali Pass. They did not realize they were unroped and, on the descent, lost sight of one another. Both sat down to sleep.

Another climber, Peter Habeler, discovered Matus 50 feet below the bodies of the German climbers. He was sitting in the snow with his gloves off; Navratil was discovered higher up. Within 45 minutes, Habeler had descended to 14,300 feet to radio for a helicopter. Unfortunately, none of the radios could transmit out that day, so Habeler's companions dragged the two Czechs down to Denali Pass.

At the pass, they were attended to by an Alaskan climber, Doug Billman, until an Army helicopter was able to land that night and evacuate the two rapidly deteriorating Czechs.

Meanwhile, Mikeska was oblivious of Matus and Navratils' problems, and had descended from the summit to the 16,100-foot camp on the Harper Glacier. The fourth climber, Novotny, died on June 17; the exact cause of his death is unknown. For some strange reason, they had been taking antibiotics to prevent altitude sickness. Dr. Charles Houston feels that some other predisposing factor (such as carbon monoxide poisoning or sleeping pills) killed Novotny and weakened the others. As in other cases, altitude impaired their judgment and led to poor decision making when the group split apart three separate times.

On June 22, 1981, a group from the North Cascades Alpine School reached the summit and returned to 17,200 feet on the West Buttress. One client was exhausted and, without telling the guides, he took 60 mg of codeine sulfate (a pain killer) and 30 mg of Dalmane (a sleeping pill). The next day the client had HACE and could barely stand; he was immediately lowered to 14,300 feet by his guides, Alan Kearney and Tim Boyer. Clearly HACE was invited by such indiscriminate drug use.

Two months later another HACE incident occurred, this time

to a Japanese climber, Yasuhiro Mitsuka. He had moved up the West Buttress at an average pace, and on the fourth morning at 11,800 feet, became quite ill with a fever of 100 degrees. His condition deteriorated that afternoon; that evening he was given two 500 mg doses of Keflex (an antibiotic). Although his condition improved briefly, he lapsed into unconsciousness at 9:30 P.M.

He died the next morning as he was being dragged to 11,000 feet. Later, an autopsy determined that the cause of death was HACE. As the climbers had been cooking in Mitsuka's tent to keep it warm, it is possible that carbon monoxide poisoning compounded Mitsuka's sickness. In all likelihood, a more immediate descent might have saved his life. (The previous HACE fatality occurred in 1974, also to a Japanese climber, at 12,800 feet on the West Buttress; details are lacking.)

On May 18, 1982, a Mountain Trip client, John Stolpman, began to experience HACE symptoms at 18,000 feet on the Northwest Buttress, after an average ascent rate of 12 days. He suffered from loss of coordination, extreme lassitude, and could not walk a straight line.

The guide radioed Dr. Peter Hackett at the 14,300-foot camp for advice. Hackett recommended that Stolpman take Diamox, receive an oxygen airdrop, and that a ground rescue team assist.

At 10:30 the next morning, the guide reported that Stolpman's condition had deteriorated. Oxygen was airdropped and a rescue team started over from 17,200 feet on the West Buttress. At some point, the guide let two clients climb to the North Peak while he was evacuating Stolpman. When the oxygen regulator froze, Stolpman's condition deteriorated rapidly and he took numerous falls without self-arresting. After the rescue team reached the party, they fixed 1,000 feet of rope and helped

58

Stolpman down. He was given more oxygen and his condition improved when he reached 17,200 feet on the West Buttress.

The following day, the rescue team assisted Stolpman down the West Buttress, while the guide and the rest of the party remained at 17,200 feet. Hackett felt that the use of oxygen eliminated the need for a major helicopter evacuation. As demonstrated in other cases, a client's fate rests upon the judgment of his guide. In this instance, it is curious that the guide allowed two of his clients to split apart and climb the North Peak. Time after time on Denali, separated parties such as this have come to grief. This group was fortunate; it had support from Hackett, a rescue team, the National Park Service and Talkeetna Air Taxi.

Every climber reacts differently in an emergency situation. With the Czechs, Demmel and Kroh, McCartney, Prentice and Mountain Trip, it is interesting to note that medical problems took second place to reaching the summit. Certainly with HACE, this attitude is dangerous because a victim deteriorates so rapidly. Also, parties that split up on a mountain further reduce their capability for self-evacuation.

On June 1, 1987, Hubert Eggert and Karl Waldmann repeated the error peculiar to German climbers: they didn't acclimatize properly and attempted the summit within six days of their arrival on Denali. At 19,200 feet, Eggert turned back while Waldmann went to the summit; both returned to 17,200 feet safely.

The next morning, Eggert was semiconscious and breathing heavily. He was administered oxygen, found in the nearby Park Service rescue cache. A Bavarian team helped lower Eggert down the rescue gully to 14,300 feet. That afternoon, Eggert was given more oxygen and Decadron. His condition stabilized overnight and he was helicoptered off in the morning.

59

At Humana Hospital in Anchorage, Dr. Peter Hackett diagnosed both severe HAPE and HACE. Eggert had read the German translation of the National Park Service mountaineering booklet and watched the German-language version of a slide presentation in Talkeetna before his climb—both warned of the dangers of rapid, unacclimatized ascents.

Three years later, an American team reacted in a more self-sufficient fashion. On May 18, 1990, Becky Goodenough and her group spent a week climbing to the 14,300-foot camp. Since Goodenough had experienced headaches and dizziness lower down, she took 500 mg of Diamox before going to sleep.

The next morning she was vomiting, dizzy, had a severe headache and ataxia (she could not walk heel to toe). She started taking Decadron, and by 3 P.M. began walking down with oxygen. At 11,200 feet, she felt better and continued out to the landing strip.

Potentially, one more day spent at 14,300 feet could have resulted in a litter evacuation or a helicopter rescue. Her (and her team's) immediate reaction to HACE is a lesson all climbers should note.

Nearly a month later, a three-man, inexperienced Japanese team left 17,200 feet for the summit after spending 19 days on Denali. Atuhiro Onodera—who had felt sick upon his arrival at 17,200 feet three days earlier—could not continue higher than 19,000 feet because of his loss of balance, headache and shortness of breath. His two partners left him and continued up: a solo American climber assisted the ataxic Onodera back down to camp.

For the next two days, Onodera ate and drank very little, and had difficulty walking. Another expedition told the team they had to descend immediately, so after administering oxygen to Onodera, he was lowered down the rescue gully to 14,300 feet.

Park Ranger Scott Gill observed Onodera fall while trying to walk heel to toe, so he was given oxygen for another 45 minutes. After one night, he improved enough to walk back down the mountain unassisted.

Ideally, Onodera should have descended when he felt sick, after his first night at 17,200 feet. He should not have attempted the summit. Furthermore, his partners made a gross error in judgment by leaving him alone at 19,000 feet with ataxia and classic HACE symptoms. If this party had been alone on the mountain, Onodera would have perished.

In conclusion, the heel-to-toe test is a sure way to detect HACE in ailing climbers. If the victim can't walk a straight line, there are three immediate courses of action: descend, descend, descend. If oxygen is available, use it; however, the victim's condition will often deteriorate when the bottle runs out. Decadron, either oral or injectable, should be carried by all climbers and given when loss of coordination develops—but only in conjunction with descent.

SUMMARY: HIGH ALTITUDE CEREBRAL EDEMA

DATE	NAME	ROUTE & ELEVATION OF INCIDENT	COMMENTS
6/9/78	HICKSON	W BUTTRESS 18300	STOPPED DIAMOX
8/25/78	PRENTICE	W BUTTRESS 17200	SEVERE HEADACHES LOST SLEEPING BAG, DELAYED DESCENT
6/9/79	KROH	W BUTTRESS SUMMIT	ILL-PREPARED, FAST ASCENT, PARTY SPLIT
6/23/79	KRUDENER	W BUTTRESS 17200	AVERAGE ASCENT RATE
6/28/79	HAMATANI	SW FACE 16200	FAST ASCENT
6/12/80	MATUS NAVRATIL NOVOTNY	HARPER 19300 & 16100	PARTY SPLIT POOR JUDGMENT
6/21/81	MCCARTNEY	SW FACE 19600	FAST ASCENT, 4 DAYS WITHOUT FOOD OR WATER
6/22/81	N CASCADES ALPINE SCHOOL	W BUTTRESS 17200	INDISCRIMINATE DRUG USE
8/8/81	MITSUKA	W BUTTRESS 11800	AVERAGE ASCENT RATE
5/18/82	STOLPMAN	NW BUTTRESS 18000	PARTY SPLIT
6/16/86	LEE JONG KWAN, CHUNG SEOUNG KWON	CASSIN RIDGE 19700	TOO FAST
6/1/87	HUBERT EGGERT	W BUTTRESS 17200	TOO FAST
6/3/88	HYN YOUNG CHUNG, CHUNG KWON LEE	CASSIN 18300	STROKE, UNACCLIMATIZED
5/19/90	BECKY GOODENOUGH	W BUTTRESS 14300	EXEMPLARY REACTION
6/14/90	ATUHIRO ONODERA	W BUTTRESS 17200	INADEQUATE RESPONSE

HOW EVACUATED	RESULT	RESCUED BY	GOVERNMENT COST
HELICOPTER	RECOVERED	ARMY	*
HELICOPTER	RECOVERED	ARMY	*
HELICOPTER	RECOVERED	ARMY	$975
AIRPLANE	RECOVERED	HUDSON AIR SERVICE	NONE
HELICOPTER WINCH	RECOVERED	ARMY	$5218
HELICOPTER	FROSTBITE, ONE DEATH	ARMY & ERA, EVERGREEN HELICOPTER	$1616
ON FOOT, SLEDDED TO LANDING STRIP	CONCUSSION, BROKEN WRIST, IMMERSION FOOT	TALKEETNA AIR TAXI, EVERGREEN HELICOPTER	$1745.10
ON FOOT, SLEDDED TO LANDING STRIP	RECOVERED		NONE
SLEDDED TO LANDING STRIP	DEATH		NONE
ON FOOT	RECOVERED	NPS, TALKEETNA AIR TAXI	*
DRAGGED OFF	RECOVERED	VERN TEJAS, WOLFGANG WIPPLER, NPS, ERA HELICOPTERS	$23141
RESCUE GULLY LOWER & HELICOPTER	RECOVERED	SOLOY HELICOPTERS	$3435
HELICOPTER WINCH	RECOVERED	ARMY	$12943
ON FOOT	RECOVERED	SELF	NONE
LOWERED DOWN RESCUE GULLY, ON FOOT	RECOVERED	OTHER TEAMS	NONE

*INDICATES INFORMATION NOT AVAILABLE

63

C H A P T E R

F r o s t b i t e

Everything was cold, even our souls.
We were drawing heavily on all our
Himalayan experience just to survive
and it was a respectful pair that
finally stood on the summit ridge.

Dougal Haston in
THE AMERICAN ALPINE JOURNAL 1977

ll of Alaska plunged below my feet. It was March 7,
1982. The wind chill brought the temperature to 100
degrees below zero. I crawled up the last 100 yards of
the Cassin Ridge sharing the characteristics of countless
Denali frostbite victims: altitude sick, severely dehydrated and
summit bound. I could feel an icy numbness on my middle toe
that was caused by my swollen, sprained ankle. The toe,
however, seemed the least of my worries.

Mike Young, shocked by my lack of progress, helped me with
my pack for the last 50 feet. He had frostbite on his nose,
thumbs and two big toes. Our appetite had dwindled because of
the altitude and, more importantly, we both had drunk very
little; Roger Mear may have been unscathed because he had
been drinking more. We were all uptight, shouting at one
another, preoccupied with the wind picking up and blowing us
off the mountain.

Nonetheless, our gear was excellent. Gore-Tex Thinsulate
suits over pile suits. Neoprene overboots with strapless Footfang

crampons (straps result in cold fingers and constrict circulation to the toes). Loose-fitting double plastic boots with "aveolite" foam inners. And polypropylene socks inside of coated nylon vapor barrier socks beneath two pair of thick wool socks. Yet gear is secondary to body maintenance, because if you don't take care of yourself, the best equipment in the world can't prevent frostbite. Particularly on Denali.

After completing our ascent of the Cassin Ridge, we hustled down the West Buttress. Two days later, frostbite blisters, or blebs, formed on Mike's big toes and on my middle toe. We walked the last miles quickly and then tried to stay off our feet while we waited a long eight days for a bush pilot.

Neither of us suffered any serious tissue damage. Dr. Mills, who examined my feet in Anchorage, diagnosed immersion foot. In recent years, because of the popularity of vapor barrier socks, Mills has seen an upsurge in immersion foot. He believes that vapor barrier socks can be a liability for climbers with unusually sweaty feet. He stressed the importance of drying one's feet every night and of taking off the vapor barrier socks. Mills also mentioned the possibility that neoprene socks might expand at altitude and thus cause circulation constriction. Add to this the possibility of peripheral edema—a swelling of the feet at altitude—and the likelihood of frostbite becomes even greater.

A common misconception is that good gear alone will prevent frostbite. Loose-fitting double boots with overboots help but, again, the overall body maintenance is crucial. Proper fluid intake is the most important factor. Diet, proper clothing, good acclimatization, warm sleeping conditions and avoidance of bad weather summit days are also important. Most climbers who suffer from frostbite aren't victims of the cold so much as their own poor body maintenance.

For instance, on June 25, 1981, a South Buttress group, guided by Michael Covington, reached the summit. Two days later, three of their tents were destroyed by an intense storm accompanied by drifting snow. Covington then located a crevasse where the group took shelter.

One of the clients, Nick Gilman, complained of being cold and hypothermic. Covington noticed that he was shivering uncontrollably and was not wearing overboots or gaitors. Although Gilman was asked repeatedly to put on his overboots, he never did. Covington also noticed that Gilman's boots were full of ice but, when asked about his feet, Gilman replied that they were okay. He warmed up after digging in the crevasse.

On June 28, assistant guide Steve Gall observed that Gilman was concerned about his feet and noticed that Gilman's right foot was very white. Gilman said his foot was numb but okay. The group had only slept for ten hours in a 74-hour period.

Gilman was hospitalized and lost portions of his toes. Covington felt that Gilman had acted with little or no concern for his feet during most of the climb and had repeatedly ignored Covington's warnings. The other nine members of the group, who were subjected to the same conditions, had no incidence of frostbite.

A year later, in July 1982, Akimichi Matsunaga wore only a light cap, without a hood, during his summit climb. The temperature was 20 degrees below zero and there was a 20-mph wind. His right ear was treated for frostbite at the thermal unit of Providence Hospital in Anchorage.

A month later, 54-year-old Miri Ercolani was trapped in a cave for three days by a windstorm at 10,000 feet on the West Buttress. Although she ate and drank adequate amounts of food and water, she never removed her plastic double boots.

When the storm ended, she continued down to the landing

strip and was flown out to Talkeetna. When she removed her boots, after wearing them continuously for five days, she discovered that both big toes were badly frostbitten. She was treated in Providence Hospital.

Climbers should take their boots off every night so that they can inspect their feet, dry them and change into dry socks. Amid the various stresses imposed by solo climbs such as Ercolani's, proper care of the feet is often overlooked. This is particularly true of the harder routes, like the Cassin, because of the technical difficulties imposed, the limited retreat options and the trend towards quick, alpine-style climbing.

In July 1982, three Scottish climbers started up the Cassin without a tent. One of the group, John Murphy, lost his sleeping pad above the Japanese Couloir. Because their bottles were freezing, they drank little water above 16,000 feet. They never removed their inner boots, which became wet from perspiration, and wore only gaitors over their boots. On the summit day, they moved slowly because of Robin Clothier's altitude sickness. The temperature at the summit was 35 degrees below zero and it was calm.

The group descended to 10,000 feet on the West Buttress where Clothier and Murphy were stopped by painful frostbite blisters. They borrowed a radio but couldn't transmit to Talkeetna. Luckily, they were able to contact a helicopter rented by a *Good Morning America* television film crew who were in search of a dramatic Denali story. They were evacuated by the film crew and the timely rescue was broadcast on nationwide television. Both Clothier and Murphy were hospitalized; after the initial examination, it appeared that Clothier would lose parts of his left toes.

When I interviewed Murphy after the climb, his attitude towards the mountain was one of nonchalance. He felt that the conditions on Denali were not nearly as severe as those he was accustomed to in Scotland, and that it was not nearly as cold. One could speculate that this attitude may have contributed to Murphy and Clothier suffering frostbitten feet. Climbing tentless on the Cassin was a big mistake as there are no possibilities for caving above 14,500 feet. The Scots might have fared better if they had insulated their water bottles, removed their inner boots and not lost a sleeping pad. (In recent years, climbers have found it easier to acclimatize high on the West Buttress and then drop back to climb the Cassin. See 1982 *American Alpine Journal*, pp. 21–28.)

Many climbers, such as the Scots, who wear gaitors with no insulation in the sole of the boot, suffer from frostbitten feet. Cold can be conducted to the foot by the steel shanks in the boots and crampons as well as by the below-surface snow. If you add to this altitude sickness, frostbite becomes inevitable.

In May 1977, a Mountain Trip guided expedition left for the summit from 17,000 feet. The temperature was 30 degrees below zero. At Denali Pass, they turned back because two of the clients, Swanson and Duffy, had altitude sickness; both had been sick earlier on the mountain. Another client, Robert Larson, who wore double ski boots with gaitors and neoprene socks, had cold feet all day.

Two days later, at 14,000 feet, Larson's toes blistered. When a radio call for a helicopter was unsuccessful, he was helped down to 10,000 feet. Meanwhile, his frostbite blisters had thawed and the walking caused the skin to tear away. He skied the rest of the way to the landing strip. As Swanson's fingers had become frostbitten during the summit attempt, both climbers were flown out immediately.

Although air evacuation of frostbite victims is sometimes done from 10,000 feet, it's a tossup between compounding the frostbite damage further by walking out an additional nine miles or of jeopardizing the pilot. Long periods of foul weather, however, often dictate that frostbite victims either walk or be dragged to the landing strip at 7,000 feet. Many climbers simply hurry back to the landing strip before blisters develop or thawing begins and never report their frostbite.

On May 16, 1981, Alan Jennings suffered frostbitten feet while walking to Denali Pass wearing boots and gaitors. Within two days, his feet had thawed and he walked down to 10,200 feet. An air evacuation was requested, but the weather was bad for two days. On May 25, he walked to the landing strip, was flown out and admitted to Providence Hospital with frostbite on four toes.

Two weeks later, Gary Selner left for the summit from 16,500 feet on the West Rib. He began the climb with cold feet, wearing double gaitors. He had constant trouble keeping his feet warm. At 19,000 feet, he turned back because he had difficulty staying warm in the high winds. He also knew that something was wrong with his feet. The next day, when he and his party tried to descend to 14,300 feet on the West Buttress, they were stopped by a whiteout. The following day, they descended to 12,500 feet.

On June 10, three days after getting frostbite, Selner had trouble descending and radioed the landing strip from 8,000 feet with a request for help. A National Park Service patrol of four, plus seven additional volunteers, dragged him to the landing strip in a sled. From here, he was flown out to Providence Hospital in Anchorage.

Selner should not have tried to reach the summit with cold feet. A recommended course of action for summit-bound climbers with cold feet is to rewarm the feet on a partner's stomach.

If the feet don't warm up within an hour of leaving for the summit, it is likely that frostbite will occur.

The final diagnosis of frostbite may overlook initial, nonfreezing tissue damage from immersion foot caused by vapor barrier socks. "Exposure is of many hours or days, and the result is an injury noted for its extensive edema, pain and slow recovery. . . ." (William J. Mills, Jr., M.D., *Alaska Medicine*, March 1973, p. 28.) Immersion (trench) foot may invite and compound later frostbite injury.

At midnight on June 21, 1980, a guided party left Denali Pass for the summit. The temperature on top was 35 degrees below zero. When they returned at 9 A.M. on June 22, one client, Wolfgang Meiers, noticed that he had frostbitten all of his toes. Although his feet had felt cold during the ascent to the summit, he didn't stop to warm them. He wore double boots, gaitors and plastic bags over his feet.

Assistant guide Nick Parker brought Meiers down to 17,200 feet on the West Buttress, while the rest of the party continued their traverse down the Muldrow Glacier. The next day, Parker and Meiers walked down to 14,300 feet. Meiers wore vapor barrier boots to provide room for his swollen toes. During the descent, his toes broke open, making him a litter case. Parker radioed out for a helicopter, but poor weather delayed the evacuation for three days. Meiers took Emperin 3 for pain and Ampicillin to prevent infection. On June 28, he was flown out from 14,300 feet. He eventually lost two toes and pieces of the eight remaining toes.

Climbers who lack cold-weather experience, such as many clients on guided trips, often overlook the loss of sensation in their feet. They are seldom aware of the seriousness of frostbite, and are reluctant to impose on the group by stopping to warm up their numb toes. It is possible that Meiers did not dry his feet every night, which could have contributed to the seriousness of his frostbite. The majority of frostbite cases on Denali occur on the summit day or at a high camp where the altitude tends to affect climbers' health and make them susceptible to cold injuries.

In 1978, two Japanese climbers bivouacked at Denali Pass because they were too exhausted to return to 17,200 feet after their summit climb. Kohji Abe wore double boots with overboots while Koh Sato wore only double boots. Sato suffered frostbite, but made it down under his own power; Abe was unscathed, probably because he wore overboots.

In 1980, members of the Boulder-Jackson expedition asked Mike McComb why he wasn't wearing overboots for his summit attempt. He replied that his "fingers got too cold when putting them on." After telling another expedition that they planned to camp as high on the mountain as they could, McComb and one other climber left in the afternoon from 17,200 feet on the West Buttress.

At 19,000 feet, they dug a snow trench and covered it with a tent fly. The weather turned very bad, with blinding snow, low visibility and cold temperatures. (This same night a German couple, Loibl and Huschke, sat down and died 300 feet above McComb.) The storm continued into the morning and there was heavy spindrift inside their trench. McComb found snow in both his outer and inner boots when he put them on for the descent. He froze his feet while walking down to the 17,200-foot camp, continued descending to 14,300 feet that night and was evacuated by helicopter the following afternoon.

High-altitude bivouacs erode one's judgment and one's capacity to withstand the cold. If McComb had used overboots and slept with his boots next to his body, his frostbite might have been prevented.

A climber in a storm on Denali. *Jonathan Waterman*

In recent years, most climbers on Denali seem to prefer lightweight double plastic boots to heavier leather boots that conduct cold through their steel shanks, and freeze solid when wet. In the winter of 1978, before plastic boots were available, four climbers elected to wear leather rather than vapor barrier boots on the Muldrow Glacier route.

Two separate storms below 17,000 feet ruined their tents, then an earthquake released an avalanche from the Harper Icefall that destroyed their snow cave beneath Karstens Ridge. The temperatures ranged from 32 degrees above zero to 37 below with a constant wind. (Cold northern winds have plagued all winter expeditions on Denali.)

During a hard day of climbing from 14,500 to 15,900 feet, one of the group, Fred Barstad, overexerted himself while cutting blocks for the snow cave. He froze his toes, despite wearing overboots.

The next morning, when Barstad announced that he was going to descend, one member of the group argued with him to continue. Barstad and Dan Knight then radioed for an evacuation; after a minor crevasse fall, they began to descend. The other two climbers, Ettore Negri and Ulf Bjornberg, stayed at the high camp.

After three days of bad flying weather, Barstad and Knight were evacuated by helicopter from 9,500 feet. Meanwhile, Negri had fallen into a crevasse with a heavy pack on, but managed to get out. When Negri and Bjornberg requested a flight out from McGonagall Pass, the request was denied because they weren't seriously in need of an evacuation; they then skied out to Kantishna.

Negri had superficial frostbite and lost some toenails; Barstad suffered more serious tissue damage. It is interesting to note that Barstad had no insulation in his overboots, while Negri had

76

some. Bjornberg and Knight, who had the most insulation, suffered the least amount of frostbite. Barstad's frostbite was caused by indadequate overboots and probable dehydration.

On the 1967 winter ascent, the team wore vapor barrier mouse boots. Despite being trapped for six days at 18,200 feet in 50-below-zero temperatures, their frostbite was relatively minor. The vapor barrier boots are not rigid and impose definite limitations on any technical climbing. Crampons that are tightly strapped to these soft boots can restrict circulation, and socks have to be changed regularly in order to keep one's feet dry. With only a few exceptions, however, these boots have had an excellent track record on Denali.

The most common incidents of frostbite are those that affect the feet. This is due to the difficulty of removing boots to check circulation and initiate warming. Ears and noses are frostbitten only rarely. Fingers are only frostbitten occasionally, under unusual circumstances, because they are much easier to warm up than feet.

In June 1977, two Italian climbers spent three days on the Messner Couloir in deep snow and bad weather. (All other parties have spent only one day on this route.) Although Antonio Klingendrath's gloves were inadequate, he continued up the route in a bad storm; as a result, he suffered frostbite on his hands. The two Italians descended from 19,600 to 17,200 feet, where other climbers took care of them. Klingendrath, who refused a helicopter evacuation, was helped down to 11,000 feet by Park Rangers; from here the two Italians continued alone to the landing strip.

In 1981, a climber descending the West Buttress, after traversing from the South Buttress, suffered frostbite on his fingers while adjusting his crampons. He also froze his toes. In 1982, during a bitterly cold April and May, I saw many climbers return to Talkeetna with frostbite blebs on their fingers and faces. One climber was a competent guide who had waited two weeks in a snow cave for the weather to clear. The selfless behavior required of good guides when dealing with inexperienced clients can be exhausting, and often leads to the guides' physical and mental deterioration; this can predispose them to frostbite.

One of the most tragic frostbite victims was Barney Dennen. On June 26, 1982, he became restless in the "carnival atmosphere" of the 14,300-foot West Buttress camp and at 1 P.M. began soloing an ice slope up the West Buttress. He finished climbing the 45-degree ice at 8 P.M. and began walking along the ridge crest toward the West Buttress fixed line in a whiteout. He immediately broke a cornice, fell free for 50 feet and then slid 500 feet down the north side of the ridge.

Unhurt, but exhausted, he dug a snow cave with an ice hammer while wearing only ragged silk gloves. During the fall, his pack containing mittens, windpants and a down parka had been torn away from him. A windstorm developed and spindrift avalanches swept over the entrance to the cave. His fingers became frozen and he alternately put them in his crotch and his mouth to thaw.

The next morning he climbed to the ridge crest, but was forced to his hands and knees by a strong wind. He was unable to use his frostbitten hands on the fixed line, so he wrapped his arms around the rope in order to descend. His climbing partner and two members of the High Latitude Research Project (HLRP) helped him down to the heated research tent at 14,300 feet, where his hands were thawed and he was given morphine for the pain.

The next day, Dennen was helicoptered off the mountain with three injured German clients, two of whom had suffered frost-

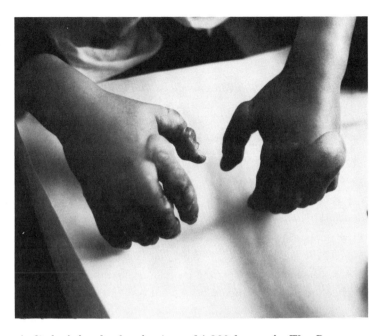

A climber's hands after thawing at 14,300 feet on the West Buttress.
DR. HOLM NEUMANN

bitten fingers in the same windstorm during a bivouac at 17,400 feet. Dennen spent weeks in the hospital and had most of his fingers amputated. He was 19 and his passion in life had been rock climbing.

That crowded carnival atmosphere at 14,300 feet may have led Dennen to underestimate the mountain. An earlier start, particularly with an obvious storm building, might have offered him better odds in pursuing a pastime on Denali that is inherently dangerous; cornices, crevasses and storms give soloists little margin for error.

Boldness on Denali usually has a price. This was also true for Mark Hesse, who made a remarkable solo ascent of the South Face in May 1982, four weeks before Dennen's accident.

In 1979, Hesse's fingers had become frostbitten while he was on the Cassin Ridge. Because he had crushed his fingers in a quarter-ton press, he was predisposed to frostbite. Just before his solo climb, he helped his brother, John, up to 12,000 feet on the West Buttress, but both turned back when John developed a sore shoulder from his crutch; he was an amputee with only one leg.

Hesse spent seven and a half days on the South Face, with two open bivouacs. On the seventh day, when he was sick from the altitude, he froze his fingers. At noon the next day he reached the summit in stormy weather. He then descended to 17,200 feet on the West Buttress, where other climbers fed him. That night, someone helped carry his pack down to 14,300 feet where Dr. Peter Hackett thawed his fingers at the HLRP tent.

The next day Hesse walked down to 10,000 feet with one of the doctors. The HLRP group and the National Park Service recommended that he ride a dog sled from 10,000 feet down to the landing strip. Hesse felt that the 50-minute, $150 sled ride was more frightening than his solo climb.

80

Mark Hesse after his South Face climb, being flown to the hospital.
JONATHAN WATERMAN

The decision to evacuate frostbitten climbers is never an easy one to make. It takes days, even in a hospital, to evaluate the severity of a frostbite injury. On the mountain, aside from the ethical ramifications of flying out ambulatory victims, high-altitude skiplane landings are risky. Although many climbers complained about the presence of a dog-sled operation on the West Buttress that summer, it was fortunate for Hesse that he had the option of using it. Perhaps due to the excellent medical treatment and the rapid evacuation, Hesse's frostbite did not involve tissue damage.

It is still not clear whether Hesse really needed to be evacuated. Will other frostbitten climbers, doctors or rangers cry dog sled or helicopter at the next sign of frostbite? Have climbers become less responsible with the knowledge that evacuations are possible?

In 1979, there were no research camps or dog-sled operations on the mountain. That year a climber with an old crushed finger injury walked down from the Cassin to the landing strip without bothering anyone about his frozen fingers. Frostbite is the most common, and least reported, accident on the mountain.

Several years later, alongside the Cassin Ridge, Bryan Becker and Rolf Graage started up an unclimbed route on the Southwest Face. They had brought too few ice screws and accidentally left their second rope in Talkeetna. It was May 23rd, 1983. Some very difficult climbing followed, until they reached a good ledge at 14,500 feet on May 28. That night snow and 80-mph winds ripped across their bivouac site; since they had lost a pole to their tent, their shelter was inadequate for melting water or cooking.

The next day Graage felt his feet numbing, but he did not rewarm them. The following morning, his feet felt like blocks of ice; he still did not try warming, let alone, thawing them.

They started climbing again on June 1. Although three toes on each of Graage's feet were frozen, he had no problem climbing; Becker's feet were fine because he had taken the trouble to rub his feet during the long stormy bivouac. Now consumed with the greater problems of survival at altitude and increasing cold, Graage didn't bother to take off his boots or look at his feet again. His frozen feet soon became very awkward while climbing.

Six days later, they intersected the Cassin Ridge, bivouacked at 20,000 feet because of the high winds, then limped down the West Buttress. When I met them at 17,200 feet, Graage was weaving back and forth—Becker was carrying both packs. Graage was severely dehydrated and couldn't talk. His toes were swollen, red and raw, with the toenails and skin sloughing off.

Becker and I lowered Graage down the rescue gully to 14,300 feet, where Dr. Peter Hackett dressed his feet. The unappreciative Graage was flown out to Anchorage that evening.

The neophytic Graage would have been spared a lot of grief and tissue loss if Becker taught him about hydration and foot maintenance, as well as placing their feet on one another's stomachs, which any other Denali guide would have done for a young client. And, as previously mentioned, few climbers escape a 20,000-foot bivouac unscathed.

During this same time period, another client frostbit his toes on the West Buttress. On May 23, while being guided by Rainier Mountaineering, Inc., Hansen lacked the experience to know that he needed to stop and warm them.

When he returned to 17,200 feet, he took off his boots and discovered that three of this toes were black with frostbite. Although Hansen could have walked out, another badly injured climber was being flown out from 14,300 feet, so he caught a

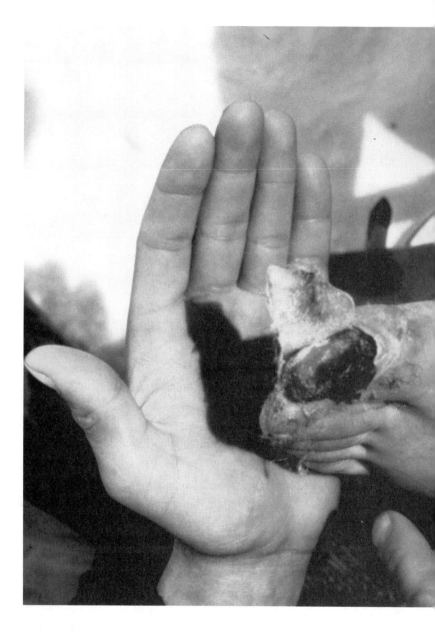

Rolf Graage's frostbitten foot. *JONATHAN WATERMAN*

Brian Becker tending the frostbitten Rolf Graage.
JONATHAN WATERMAN

ride in order that his frostbite damage be minimized. He was billed for the flight by Talkeetna Air Taxi.

Clients, or climbers inexperienced in dealing with sub-zero cold, have to learn about nonconstricting boots, proper hydration and rewarming procedures. Climbers, in particular guides in charge of clients, must anticipate the surmountable inconvenience and potential ego hang-ups involved in halting a summit push so that members can warm their feet on each other stomachs. Unattended numb toes on a summit day are a sure invitation to frostbite.

Five days later, at 19,000 feet, Sam Foster removed his vapor barrier gloves several times while adjusting his face mask. It was 20 degrees below zero with a 25-mph wind. Shortly afterward, he turned back to the 17,200-foot camp. Later that evening he noticed he had frostbitten six fingertips.

Ultimately, vapor barrier gloves are inappropriate for Denali. The moisture trapped on your hands makes the gloves cold, a liability to fingers when the gloves are pulled off and wet skin in exposed to the cold.

Another frostbite concept was illustrated on Michael Beiser's South Buttress climb. On May 31, 1984, Beiser went to the summit; there was little wind and the temperature was 25 degrees below zero. Beiser wore lightweight super gaitors and felt inner boots that were slightly damp; his fluid intake that day was half a quart.

During the descent, he experienced pain, then realized he had frozen his big toe. The toe swelled and turned black overnight, but he walked out to base camp unassisted.

Probably dry inner boots, better hydration and overboots would have worked in Beiser's favor. One final note is that Beiser chewed tobacco. Like cigarettes, tea and coffee, tobacco is a vasoconstrictor that restricts blood flow to the fingers and toes.

On May 6, 1985, a fast-moving storm descended upon the guided Vail Denali group while they were carrying loads to 13,600 feet on Karstens Ridge (Muldrow Glacier Route). The winds began knocking people off their feet. One gust blew Greg Kemp's pack off Ted Billings' back (Billings, the guide, had already cached his pack above and was helping Kemp.) Soon another pack was blown away. The next gust pulled out the fixed line and caused Billings and others to fall several hundred feet, stopping short of a 3,000-foot plunge off the Harper Icefall.

Billings managed to pull a tent over himself and two others while the rest of the group did the same, bracing themselves against the 100-mph wind that blew all night. No one could move. Outside, clinging to the remnants of the fixed line, his arm braced around an ice ax, Greg Kemp was beyond everyone's reach. His Gore-Tex Thinsulate gloves had gotten wet during the day; without his pack or spare mittens, he frostbit four fingers.

Fortunately, by morning, the wind abated. A Chicago Mountaineering Club group camped below plied the Vail Denali group with shelter, food and hot drinks. The team had lost two packs and vital group gear. Consequently, Greg and Paul Kemp were helicoptered out later that day. The Vail Denali group proceeded with the long walk out the Wonder Lake Road.

Although all gloves are inferior to mittens with windshells, even mittens might not have prevented Kemp's fingers from freezing. Billings' postclimb report read: ". . . a matter of being in the wrong place at the the wrong time, it could have happened to any experienced expedition. I would try not to get separated from my pack." The group was not the first to learn that on

Denali, a beautiful morning can quickly degenerate into a nightmarish afternoon.

Nine days later, on the West Buttress, James Raymond and Ronald Uhle reached the summit. Raymond's feet were cold and both men drank only a half quart of water that day.

When they returned to 17,200 feet, Uhle did not take off his vapor barrier socks, while, for the fourth day in a row, Raymond did not remove his inner boots. In the morning, Uhle discovered frost on his white waxy toes; Raymond found his big toes purple with frostbite blebs the size of nickels. They both warmed their feet with warm water bottles and drank some water. They descended to the 14,300-foot medical camp on May 17. Raymond's toes were determined to be more seriously frostbitten than Uhle's; after taking painkillers and Rufen (an anti-inflammatory drug), they walked to the 7,000-foot landing strip.

These climbers' experience again underscores the importance of checking one's feet every evening, taking off vapor barrier socks and inner boots, and drinking plenty of fluids on summit days. Furthermore, the summit temperature was 40 degrees below zero, a typical May day, where the finest equipment (they wore neoprene overboots) makes little difference in frostbite prevention.

Meanwhile, at 17,200 feet, one-legged Sara Doherty sat out the same period of weather that Raymond and Uhle chose to summit in. At 10 P.M. on May 19, Doherty, a member of the "Tripod" team who used special crutches with sharpened ferrules, became the first amputee to reach the summit of Denali. Doherty climbed not only with calculated safety, but admirable guts.

However, a storm broke on the descent. Coming down from Denali Pass, in windchill temperatures of 40 degrees below zero, Doherty's crutches couldn't penetrate the hard ice. During the five hours it took the group to descend this 1,000-foot section, Doherty became frightened and overgripped her crutches, which probably contributed to her frostbite.

She descended to the medical camp and was diagnosed with third-degree frostbite on her thumb and first-degree frostbite on some of her fingers. Under her own considerable powers, Doherty reached the 7,000-foot landing strip on May 24.

Although her crutches were well-engineered and innovative pieces of equipment, the use of an insulated gauntlet over the crutch handles might benefit future amputees on Denali. Nonetheless, many two-legged climbers have descended in similar storms and received worse frostbite than Doherty did.

On June 9 of the same year, Bruno Garagnon shot motion pictures of his French companions reaching the summit via the West Buttress route. The temperature was zero degrees. Each time Garaganon filmed, he pulled off his mittens and worked the camera with thin silk gloves. In addition, he drank very little. When he reached Denali Pass during the descent, he noticed frostbite on all of his fingertips.

At 17,200 feet, he rewarmed his fingers. The next day, during the descent, Dr. Frank Hollingshead bandaged his fingers at the medical camp. Garagnon then continued down unassisted.

On June 15, Garagnon checked into Providence Hospital in Anchorage. He was diagnosed with first- and second-degree frostbite on all of his fingertips. Obviously, proper hydration and thicker gloves might have prevented frostbite. Furthermore, at the hospital, Garagnon remembered that his fingers had been frostnipped the first day of his climb after gas had been spilled on them.

On May 21, 1990, a German climber was involved in a similar incident. Leo Schlecter reached the 17,200-foot West

Buttress camp in a fast five days. The second night there, his butane stove leaked all over his hands in subzero conditions. The next morning, he descended to the medical camp and was advised to go to the hospital immediately. Although the details of Schlecter's recovery are unknown, the staff at Providence Hospital surmised that he would lose small portions from all his fingertips.

It should be noted that white gas, or butane gas (which liquefies in cold temperatures), assumes air temperature and must be handled with care. If liquid gas is spilled on the skin in subzero conditions, it will cause immediate frostbite.

On May 3, 1989, a Korean team—a nationality infamous for epics on the Cassin Ridge—started its climb. On May 24, Ku-Taek Shin became sick with AMS (and continued to be sick for the next five days). Rather than descend, the team continued up the Cassin Ridge, until eventually Shin contracted severe frostbite of his hands and feet.

He wore plastic double boots (with stock woolen inner boots) and supergaitors. On his hands, he wore only gloves with an insulated shell. His frostbite injury was surely compounded by dehydration, AMS and marginal equipment.

On May 28, the team reached the summit; at this point, Shin was only a helpless liability. They bivouacked at Denali Pass. On the following day, the team descended to the medical camp, where Shin's hands and feet were thawed in an antiseptic bath, and intravenous fluids were administered. As weather conditions did not permit an air evacuation, on June 1, the Koreans dragged Shin down the West Buttress on a sled. Word had gotten out in Korea that their countrymen were receiving too many evacuations from Denali (see HACE chapter), so they wanted to handle this evacuation themselves. When they reached the Northeast Fork of the Kahiltna Glacier, Shin was left outside for two days, strapped onto the litter, while his teammates recovered a cache several miles away. Finally, on June 5, Shin was flown out from the 7,000-foot landing strip. His frostbite injuries were certainly compounded by the delay in his evacuation.

Such a lack of compassion may be due to the Koreans' notion of "face." In their minds, Shin had brought great shame to the group, so they treated him like an animal. Certainly, the Koreans could have averted both Shin's frostbite and other great difficulties if they had simply preacclimatized on the West Buttress route. Finally, as no Korean team had completed the Cassin Ridge, this team was determined to complete the climb, no matter the price. Before Shin flew back to Korea, the prognosis was that eight fingers and five toes would be amputated.

Although technological advances have made high-quality, warm clothing and equipment available to every climber, frostbite continues to plague Denali climbers. Proper hydration and acclimatization, together with an aggressive attitude toward the cold, are key factors in preventing frostbite. Otherwise, nonconstrictive boots, keeping one's feet dry, avoiding spilled gas, abstaining from vasoconstrictors (tobacco, tea, coffee) and dressing properly would all help climbers to go home with their fingers and toes intact. If every expedition could meet a frostbite amputee—and witness the sense of loss, the frustrating recovery period and the medical expenses—perhaps future expeditions would understand that reaching the summit is not worth losing a single finger or toe.

SUMMARY: FROSTBITE

DATE	NAME	ROUTE & ELEVATION OF INCIDENT	COMMENTS
6/23/77	KLINGENDRATH	MESSNER COULOIR 18000	INADEQUATE GLOVES
3/13/78	BARSTAD	MULDROW 15900	OVEREXTENDED, LITTLE FOOD, INADEQUATE OVERBOOTS
6/2/78	SATO	W BUTTRESS 18300	BIVOUAC, NO OVERBOOTS
5/28/80	MCCOMB	W BUTTRESS 19000	BIVOUAC, NO OVERBOOTS
6/21/80	MEIERS	W BUTTRESS SUMMIT	NO OVERBOOTS
5/16/81	JENNINGS	W BUTTRESS 18300	NO OVERBOOTS
6/7/81	SELNER	W RIB 18000	NO OVERBOOTS
6/27/81	GILMAN	S BUTTRESS 15000	NO OVERBOOTS
3/6/82	YOUNG WATERMAN	CASSIN 19600	DEHYDRATION, ALTITUDE SICKNESS, INADEQUATE DIET
5/18/82	HESSE	S FACE 19000	DEHYDRATION
6/26/82	DENNEN	W BUTTRESS 16000	SOLO, CORNICE COLLAPSE, BIVOUAC, INADEQUATE CLOTHING
7/2/82	MATSUNAGA	W BUTTRESS SUMMIT	LIGHT HAT WITHOUT HOOD
7/23/82	ERCOLANI	W BUTTRESS 10000	LEFT BOOTS ON FOR 5 DAYS

FROSTBITE

HOW EVACUATED	RESULTED	RESCUED BY	GOVERNMENT COST
ON FOOT	FROSTBITTEN FINGERS		NONE
HELICOPTER	FROSTBITTEN TOES	NPS	$2767.20
ON FOOT	FROSTBITTEN TOES		NONE
HELICOPTER	FROSTBITTEN TOES	AKLAND HELICOPTER SERVICE	$1767.02
HELICOPTER	AMPUTATION 2 TOES, 8 DIGITS	EVERGREEN & TALKEETNA AIR TAXI	$11439.37
ON FOOT	4 FROSTBITTEN TOES		NONE
DRAGGED TO LANDING STRIP	FROSTBITTEN TOES		NONE
DRAGGED TO LANDING STRIP	PARTIAL TOE AMPUTATION		NONE
ON FOOT	MINOR TISSUE DAMAGE		NONE
DOG SLED	MINOR TISSUE DAMAGE		NONE
HELICOPTER	AMPUTATION OF ALL FINGERS	ARMY	**
ON FOOT	FROSTBITTEN EAR		NONE
ON FOOT	FROSTBITTEN TOES		NONE

*INDICATES INFORMATION NOT AVAILABLE
**IN 1982, THE ARMY BILLED THE NPS $67,000 FOR ALL RESCUE OPERATIONS.

93

SUMMARY: FROSTBITE

DATE	NAME	ROUTE & ELEVATION OF INCIDENT	COMMENTS
8/1/82	MURPHY CLOTHIER	CASSIN SUMMIT	NO TENT, DEHYDRATION, ALTITUDE SICKNESS, GAITORS
5/29/83	ROLF GRAAGE	SOUTHWEST FACE 14500	DEHYDRATION, NO REWARMING
5/23/83	DOUG HANSEN	W BUTTRESS 19000	NO REWARMING
5/28/83	SAM FOSTER	W BUTTRESS 19000	VAPOR BARRIER GLOVES
5/31/84	MICHAEL BEISER	S BUTTRESS 19000	DAMP INNER BOOTS, DEHYDRATION, CHEWING TOBACCO
5/6/85	GREG KEMP	MULDROW GLACIER 13000	SUDDEN STORM, INADEQUATE GLOVES
5/15/85	JAMES RAYMOND RONALD UHLE	W BUTTRESS 17200	IMPROPER BODY MAINTENANCE
5/19/85	SARAH DOHERTY	W BUTTRESS 18000	OVERGRIPPING CRUTCHES
6/9/85	BRUNO GARAGNON	W BUTTRESS ABOVE 18300	SPILLED GAS, INADEQUATE SILK GLOVES, DEHYDRATION
5/21/90	LEO SCHLECTER	W BUTTRESS 17200	SPILLED GAS
5/24/89	KU-TAEK SHIN	CASSIN RIDGE 17000	AMS, DEHYDRATION, EVACUATION DELAY

HOW EVACUATED	RESULTED	RESCUED BY	GOVERNMENT COST
HELICOPTER	MINOR TISSUE DAMAGE, TISSUE LOSS FROM ALL LEFT-FOOT TOES	*	NONE
TALKEETNA AIR TAXI	LOSS OF TISSUE	NATIONAL PARK SERVICE	NONE
TALKEETNA AIR TAXI	RECOVERY	SELF	NONE
TALKEETNA AIR TAXI	FIRST-DEGREE FROSTBITE	SELF	NONE
FOOT	RECOVERED	SELF	NONE
HELICOPTER	AMPUTATION OF MIDDLE FINGER	NPS, ALASKA HELICOPTER	$6416
FOOT	THIRD DEGREE FROSTBITE	SELF	NONE
FOOT	THIRD-DEGREE FROSTBITE	SELF	NONE
FOOT	RECOVERED	SELF	NONE
FOOT	THIRD DEGREE FROSTBITE	SELF	NONE
SLED	AMPUTATIONS	HIS OWN TEAM	NONE

*INDICATES INFORMATION NOT AVAILABLE
**IN 1982, THE ARMY BILLED THE NPS $67,000 FOR ALL RESCUE OPERATIONS.

95

CHAPTER FIVE

Climbing Falls

*Perhaps it would have been
a wise decision
not to push our luck.*

A Climbing Instructor
on Denali

lthough the actual technical climbing on Denali is limited, many climbers forget that altitude, arctic conditions and heavy packs make 35-degree snowslopes subjectively 55 degrees.

In the following accounts of 27 falls on Denali, it is instructive to know that 21 occurred during the descent; only three happened during the climb up, while four falls were below 15,000 feet. Otherwise, the greatest number of falls occur while climbers descend from Denali Pass to 17,200 feet. The conclusion is that most victims fall because they have altitude sickness or hypothermia. Furthermore, sickness, exhaustion or inexperience often causes stumbles; combined with a lack of self-arrest technique or ice axes, these stumbles often result in death.

On June 2, 1972, a Ray Genet guided party reached Denali Pass, but had to turn back because of high winds and poor visibility. A short way down, the "snow gave way" underneath Dick Witte's foot; he fell ten feet, until his crampon caught, and broke his left leg. He continued to fall down the 30-degree slope for 60 feet until another client self-arrested and stopped the fall. Genet splinted Witte's leg and moved him down to the 17,200-foot camp. From here he was evacuated two days later by a gutsy helicopter pilot.

A year later, in 1973, another Genet guided party was descending below Denali Pass after their summit climb. One of the clients, Joe Wiley, was so affected by the altitude that he was unable to descend without a great deal of help. Some of the team members decided to make a faster descent: six members of the group began to slide down the slope in a self-arrest position. Greg Brown, the last person on the seven-man rope team, had not been told of this decision. After sliding 50 feet, the entire rope team lost control and slid 400 to 500 feet. Brown tumbled head over heels and suffered cuts, bruises and a concussion. That night, he was moved to 17,200 feet. The next day his condition improved and, with difficulty, he was helped to 14,300 feet where, together with another member of the team, Charles Schertz, who was uninjured, he was evacuated by an Army helicopter.

It is difficult enough for one person to perform a self-arrest. When an entire team, some of whose members are weary and sick, tries such a maneuver on a wind-packed, crevassed glacier, the results can be disastrous. Wiley should have been assisted down on the arms of the two strongest climbers.

The next known fall at Denali Pass occurred in July 1976. A five-man Austrian traverse party was descending after having reached the summit. As Ortwin Wister was having trouble breathing, the leader, Helmut Linzbichler, sent Gunter Schmidt for the doctor in a Canadian party that was below them. At about 18,800 feet, Schmidt either slipped while peering over the edge or decided to descend directly to the Canadian party;

he then fell 1,200 feet down the slope in front of the Canadians' traverse route and into a crevasse. He apparently died instantly from a broken neck. His body was never recovered. Like many other European climbers who approach the summit from the West Buttress, Schmidt carried ski poles rather than an ice ax for self-arresting.

Meanwhile, Wister, the climber with the breathing problem, recovered. Three of the Austrians went down the Muldrow Glacier route, while Linzbichler, who was unaware of Schmidt's death, descended the West Buttress to tell him that a doctor was not needed.

According to the Canadians, Schmidt had climbed to the summit quickly, had made jokes with them on top and was well acclimated. Linzbichler was evacuated by helicopter from 17,200 feet for a number of reasons: to prevent him from descending the Muldrow Glacier alone, to clarify problems with the Anchorage and Austrian press, and to notify Schmidt's next of kin.

Schmidt would have been able to self-arrest if he had carried an ice ax. Also, splitting a group up, which proved to be a mistake for the Austrians, should be avoided.

On May 11, 1980, another traverse party of four was ferrying loads to Denali Pass from 17,200 feet on the West Buttress. They were unroped, but using crampons and ice axes. On the way back down, a German climber, Gerold Herrman, stumbled and took a tumbling fall. The other three took ten minutes to reach his body in a shallow crevasse. Although they performed CPR for 30 minutes, there was no response. They eventually lowered the body to 14,300 feet where it was evacuated on May 16, together with a member of the group.

At Denali Pass, altitude sickness or variable snow conditions

Denali Pass descent, where many falls occur. *BRIAN OKONEK*

can cause climbers to stumble. If this team had been roped together, Herrman's fall might have been stopped.

In 1982, two falls in the Denali Pass area resulted in evacuations. Both were classic examples of inexperienced, poorly led climbers getting in over their heads.

The first group was brought together through a University of Alaska mountaineering class. They named their expedition "Denali 101," and used a computer and a local guide as a consultant to plan their trip.

During their first week on the glacier, two members of the group abandoned the expedition because of personality conflicts. Two weeks later, the rest of the group split in two on their way to the summit. One member of the slower group had acute mountain sickness (he collapsed and was incoherent). The others immediately radioed the National Park Service and asked about the feasibility of a helicopter evacuation. They were advised to descend and call back in an hour with a progress report. Finally, a former military officer in the team bypassed the Park Service, dialed Fort Wainwright in Anchorage on his radio telephone and convinced the Army to send helicopters for the Denali 101 rescue.

As the Chinook helicopters made their way to Talkeetna, the sick climber improved during the descent to 17,200 feet. Then a woman in the second group slipped below Denali Pass; her fall was arrested by the rest of the group she was roped into. Although she had only sprained her ankle, the team radioed a circling military plane that she had broken it. When the beleaguered team arrived at 17,200 feet, they did not solicit the advice of doctors in a nearby tent to determine whether a helicopter was necessary. However, they did try to leave the injured woman and another frostbitten man in the doctors' care while they descended. When the helicopter arrived, another

104

member of the group frostbit his feet while loading the woman aboard; he was eventually evacuated by dog sled. Of the ten people who started up Denali, two left early, one had debilitating altitude sickness and three were evacuated.

This group's high attrition rate could be attributed to their inexperience and lack of cohesiveness as a team. A group such as this should never consider splitting apart, thus weakening themselves further. Their first reaction to altitude sickness was to inquire about a helicopter rather than to descend immediately. Denali 101's origin in a college classroom was a contrived means of team selection. Ideally, an expedition should be composed of friends who have climbed together. Their initial plan to hire a guide, which was not carried out, might have given them the leadership they lacked.

Nine days later, on May 26, 1982, an 18-member Genet Expeditions guided party from the German Alpine Club left for the summit from 17,200 feet in deteriorating weather conditions. Two of the three guides remained behind because they were sick and because of a disagreement about making a summit attempt in poor weather. At Denali Pass, visibility was 20 to 30 yards with high winds, but the climbers continued. Below Kahiltna Horn, the head guide turned back with two clients, but was roped into just one of them. On the way down from Denali Pass, the unroped client fell, dropped her ice ax and slid 1,200 feet, sustaining several compression fractures of her vertebrae.

Meanwhile, the remainder of the party had turned around below the summit headwall because of the deteriorating weather conditions. One client collapsed and had to be supported all the way down. Below Denali Pass, the climbers were unroped and most of them used ski poles instead of ice axes. Three men slipped and fell in the freshly fallen snow but were unhurt. By

Assisting injured climber from Germany who fell from Denali Pass. *JONATHAN WATERMAN*

accident, they met the head guide and the two clients, but couldn't find their way back to the 17,200-foot camp because of whiteout conditions. They then spread out and bivouacked in the open. They had no shovels to dig in with, no stoves and no radio.

The next morning the weather was clear with 70- to 100-mph winds. The group made it back to 17,200 feet where they asked Ranger Roger Robinson for help. In addition to one client who suffered a back injury, all of the group were hypothermic, and two people had frostbitten fingers. Because their tents had blown down, Robinson helped the group to find shelter in caves with other climbers. The next day, when the storm had abated, they descended to 14,300 feet, where three clients were evacuated in a military helicopter along with another client who had suffered frostbite in the same storm.

This group made numerous mistakes. The disagreement over the weather should have precluded a summit attempt that day. Also, going to the summit with only one out of three guides showed poor judgment. The head guide should have brought the entire group back down, instead of allowing them to split up and proceed without a guide. All of the clients should have been roped together; they should have carried ice axes, stoves, a radio and a shovel. If the weather had been worse, this group would not have survived.

Many Germans who go to Denali underestimate both the mountain and its weather. Statistics show that, from 1973 to 1982, Germans were involved in more accidents than any other nationality. It is unfortunate that these poorly led groups continue to make the same mistakes, such as climbing unroped without ice axes in poor weather. Inevitably, they jeopardize other climbers and the pilots who must rescue them. For the next eight years, Germans and others continued to be hurt, rescued or killed with frightening regularity after falling near Denali Pass—usually without ice axes.

Falls that occur while climbers are ascending are rare. Usually, inexperienced climbers fall on 30- to 40-degree snow and ice slopes when returning from the summit with altitude sickness, exhaustion, hypothermic or in poor weather conditions. Experienced climbers, who fall on technically difficult ground, are forced to deal with the accident on their own.

At 2 A.M., on May 22, 1979, Ken Currens took a 240-foot leader fall when the snow ledge he was standing on collapsed. An ice screw 30 feet above his belayer, Jack Tackle, held the fall. They were on a steep, 60-degree to vertical variation of the South Buttress route, an unclimbed, isolated spur of the Ruth Glacier. Tackle lowered Currens to a bergschrund and rappelled down to him. Although his helmet probably prevented serious head injury, he had fractured his left femur.

Tackle gave him a pain killer, lowered him to their ice cave and skied out five miles to the Mountain House for help. At 4:30 P.M., he contacted Cliff Hudson with his CB radio and flew out with Hudson to Talkeetna to organize a rescue. He returned to the Ruth Glacier at 7:45 P.M. with Mugs Stump and Jim Logan. Four hours later, they had climbed up to the cave; at 1 A.M., they began 300-foot lowers, with Stump belaying and Logan and Tackle on the Thompson litter with Currens. At 4 A.M., they arrived at the glacier and splinted Currens' leg with two snow pickets. By 7:30 A.M., helicopter pilot, Jim Okonek, and Hudson had evacuated all four to Talkeetna.

Tackle and Currens were competent climbers doing a hard route. After the accident, they used better judgment, leadership and resourcefulness than parties five times their size have displayed on the West Buttress. Tackle could have fallen into a crevasse while skiing down for help, but he understood that risk. They did carry a radio and managed their rescue with grace under fire. Tackle came back two more times with just a single partner and finally completed the route in 1982.

Between 1970 and 1982, there were four serious falls from the West Rib. In April 1970, a four-man party made the second ascent of the West Rib. At 13,000 feet, during their descent, either Gerald Smith or John Luz slipped and pulled the other off. They fell 2,000 feet down the initial couloir to their deaths. Apparently, they were not attached to their fixed line when they slipped.

In June 1972, three Japanese women fell down the West Rib while descending from the summit. They were found dead at the 15,000-foot level by Ray Genet. It's likely that the three women were tired from their summit climb and that one of them slipped and pulled the others off the 35- to 50-degree snowslopes between 17,800 and 19,400 feet. In 1979, 1982, and 1989, similar accidents occurred in the same gully.

In May 1979, three Korean climbers left from 14,000 feet on the West Rib for the summit. (This was an unreasonably long day and the group carried no water.) Later, they radioed down that they had made the summit, but that they were very tired. According to one of the climbers, Hun-Kyu Park, the snow slipped out from under him on the descent and he fell; he expected the other two to self-arrest and stop him, but they didn't. (What Park neglected to mention after the accident was that none of the team wore crampons. This was a major mistake and the cause of the fall.) The three climbers slid approximately 2,500 feet down the gully, stopping at 15,500 feet.

Luckily, before the weather deteriorated, they were seen from 14,300 feet. Again, the tireless Denali guide, Ray Genet, together with another guide, Brian Okonek, went up to the fallen climbers. San-Don Ko was dead and Li-Kyo Lee had severe head injuries. After placing Lee in a snow cave, they lowered Park to 14,300 feet on the West Buttress. When Okonek and four others went back for Lee, he was dead.

Park was attended to by Dr. Bing at the 14,300-foot camp. Bing, who just happened to be there, kept Park's frozen feet packed in snow but thawed his hands since they were already thawing. Later the same day, Park was airlifted from 14,300 feet by a helicopter. He had a badly dislocated knee, and later lost the tips of his toes and many of the joints on his left had to frostbite. Medical attention at the 14,300-foot West Buttress camp would once again prove invaluable for climbers who fell from the West Rib; so would Brian Okonek.

In May and June 1982, Dr. Peter Hackett and Okonek were part of a team manning the High Latitude Research Project (HLRP) tent at 14,300 feet on the West Buttress. On June 4, Okonek noticed two dots in the same spot where the Koreans had been three years earlier. Okonek and Hackett reached the two climbers, Takashi Kanda and Mamoru Ida; with help from 11 other climbers, they sledded them down to their heated medical tent.

Kanda and Ida both had head injuries and were put on IV fluids and oxygen. Ida had frostbite on his hands, feet and penis. The weather remained bad until June 7. The situation became critical because ground teams couldn't make it up to the camp in the heavy snows to replenish the dwindling IV fluids needed for the injured pair. Finally, during a quick break in the clouds, Kanda and Ida were evacuated by an Army helicopter. Without the HLRP group, the two comatose Japanese would have died.

Okonek thought Ida's frostbite had developed prior to the fall and that the pair had been forced to bivouac in a storm. They probably slipped at about 18,000 feet while descending from

A comatose climber, Takashi Kanda, being rescued from the West Rib in 1982. *BRIAN OKONEK*

the summit: like previous victims suffering altitude sickness or their inability to self-arrest on the 35- to 50-degree snow. Perhaps one more acclimatization day at the 16,500-foot camp on the West Rib and sharper self-arrest skills could prevent this accident from happening to other climbers. Since five Oriental climbers have died here, those familiar with the gully's accident history named it the "Orient Express."

Ten years after the Korean disaster in the Orient Express, a memorial expedition from Korea conducted a service to eulogize Lee and Ko at the 14,300-foot camp. In the midst of their ceremony, the clouds lifted and three more bodies were spotted at the base of the now infamous chute on the West Rib.

Ranger Roger Robinson organized the body recovery. After a thorough investigation, he learned that the three British climbers—Chris Massey, John Lang and Julian Dixon—had started toward the summit on May 17, 1989. That same day, while descending the West Rib during his own attempt, volunteer Park Ranger Mark Stasik met the British at 18,300 feet. Stasik warned the leader, Massey, that "the winds are bad, it's going to be a whiteout and you can't see anything . . . you're going to have a real hard time finding your way back down."

Massey replied, "We're going to the summit, we don't care about the view."

The weather worsened, and presumably, the British fell from 18,300 feet while descending from their summit attempt many hours later. Certainly, if they had placed intermediate anchors, the fall could have been arrested—a factor affecting all of the falls from this area. In the end, however, prevention is the best protection. Worsening weather, coupled with warnings from other climbers, is all the information a sensible climber needs.

In the eighties, the West Rib has became the scene of all too many climbing falls. During the winter of 1983, on March 11,

Dr. Bill Hammel checking for a pulse on a body beneath the Orient Express. *ROGER ROBINSON*

Robert Franks and Charlie Sassara began frontpointing (unroped) down the upper snowslopes after their first winter ascent of the West Rib. Conditions were tricky: hard ice, soft corn snow, wind crust and hard snow. Both climbers were badly fatigued after their achievement. At 18,900 feet, Frank yelled "falling" and slammed into Sassara; both climbers careened down the mountain. Sassara self-arrested after 100 feet, while Frank fell 4,500 feet to his death.

Sassara descended, badly shaken, finding blood, pieces of equipment and several pieces of Frank's bones with flesh attached. Sassara made it back safely to his 17,000-foot camp. A week later, after a fruitless search for Frank, Sassara and his two surviving companions were flown out from the 7,000-foot landing strip.

Ultimately, winter climbing on Denali is an uncompromising, deadly door into eternity—regardless of a climber's ability. For instance, in the winter of 1989, three Japanese climbers, who had climbed many 8,000-meter peaks, were found dead at 17,000 feet after falling from Denali Pass. Although the autopsy stated that they died from hypothermia, the high winds probably blew them down the mountainside. Out of 19 serious attempts (climbers who got above 18,000 feet) on Denali in winter, 17 made it to the summit; but five were killed (mostly in falls) and six received acute injuries. If considering a winter climb, remember that, in addition to all of the other considerations about proper travel on steep slopes, more than half of the serious winter attempts on Denali result in death or serious injury.

On May 12, 1985, an unusual fall occurred on the West Rib when Marc Williams was anchoring his tent at 16,000 feet. He had taken off his crampons and was wearing "Forty Below" neoprene overboots; while trying to hammer in a snow picket, he slipped and fell. Apparently, the angle of the slope, the hardness of the ice and the speed of his fall prevented Williams from self-arresting with his ice hammer. He fell more than 2,000 feet to his death. Two days later, Mugs Stump and Terry Schmidt climbed to the body and lowered it to a waiting helicopter.

In conclusion, a fall from a steep tent site at the end of the day, in slippery-soled overboots, should be the waking nightmare of every climber. It is amazing that more overbooted climbers haven't fallen off Denali.

A more typical fall occurred on May 3, 1987, when Scotsman Stan Darke was descending the West Rib at 14,800 feet without a rope. While moving between fixed ropes (possibly snagging a crampon), he slipped and fell 800 feet. Fortunately, his teammates witnessed the fall, descended to him and set up a tent. Darke was unconscious, with a suspected skull fracture, labored breathing, a chest injury and multiple contusions. Late that night, Andrew Nesbit finished descending to the 7,000-foot landing strip and radioed the Park Rangers for help.

The next morning, an Army Chinook helicopter lowered a paramedic and a litter. Darke was strapped on, then the litter and the paramedic were hoisted back aboard. In the hospital, Darke remained comatose with bruised lungs, bleeding in his brain and cartilage separation in his chest.

In hindsight, it is easy to say that such falls could be avoided if one were tied into a climbing partner. The Scotsmen were unroped because they felt that a roped and belayed descent was too time consuming. But the rescue operation put a dozen different lives at various degrees of risk, cost the taxpayer $33,754, involved four different helicopters and two airplanes. It was the second of several cable-winching rescues to follow on Denali. Although these operations have worked safely so far, few people know that the helicopter pilot has an electronically fired cable cutter which he has been commanded to push if there is undue risk to his crew.

Nonetheless, even a roped descent is no guarantee of safety, as illustrated by some Japanese climbers on the Cassin Ridge in May 1974. Five members of an eight-man team had reached the summit and were rappelling back down. In the Japanese Couloir (named for the second-ascent team's variation on Riccardo Cassin's original route), two climbers rappelled down their 8 mm fixed line. When Yoshikazu Okado followed, the rope broke. He fell 800 feet and was killed.

Fixed line is now a part of a bygone era on Denali. Nevertheless, rope still festoons the Cassin like historical graffiti. In 1967, Bill Phillips fell 70 feet while rappelling on Cassin's old line, which broke. Mike Helms wrote of an incident that occurred on the Cassin in 1980. When he clipped into an old line, it broke and he fell over backwards; miraculously, however, he stopped himself in what he called the closest call he'd ever had in the mountains. Even new fixed rope must be regarded as suspect due to sharp crampons, rockfall and abrasive weather conditions.

Now, for reasons of safety and ethics, most climbers prefer to rely solely on their own climbing ropes, and to walk down the West Buttress instead of rappelling their route. In deciding whether or not to bring fixed rope, climbers must recognize their own limitations. Instead of placing fixed lines on a difficult route, consider doing an alpine-style ascent of an easier one. Too often, climbers develop an unnecessary dependence on equipment instead of relying on their own skill and good judgment. The Sourdoughs and Archdeacon Stuck never heard of fixed rope.

Now that fixed rope is seldom used on the Cassin Ridge, climbers are forced to come up with more creative means of retreat, because rappelling the route is tricky. Consequently, more than one party has traversed off at the 16,500-foot level. But, in June 1990, Michael Koshuta and Stuart Jones paid a terrible toll for this traverse. On June 9, they were overdue; after two days of inquiry, an aerial search was begun. On June 12, their bodies were sighted at 15,800 feet, near the West Rib.

Eight days later, Park Rangers Scott Gill and Doug Chabot climbed over to the victims. Although they were roped, they had placed no protection between them; this might have prevented the fall. They had only a small bag of food, were out of fuel, and their tent was missing some poles. The bodies were left on the mountain because of the difficulty and danger of an evacuation from 40-degree ice slopes. To date, including Jones and Koshuta, 31 bodies have been left on the mountain.

When Gill got back to Talkeetna, he developed Jones' film, which showed no pictures of the pair reaching the summit. In all likelihood, they had simply run out of food or gotten sick while waiting out the bad weather in early June, and then decided that the traverse was their easiest escape. This 40-pitch traverse off the Cassin Ridge should not be underestimated, and is only recommended for strong climbers in good weather, with stable snow conditions.

On July 13, 1973, after climbing the South Peak, a National Outdoor Leadership School (NOLS) group attempted the North Peak from 17,600 feet on the Harper Glacier. While waiting to use a fixed line at the top of a couloir, one student took off his pack, anchored it to his ice ax and climbed up to a ropemate to ask a favor. He slipped and, without his ax, couldn't self-arrest; he pulled the other three climbers 800 feet down the couloir. (The students were "not terribly proficient at self-arrest techniques" and the snow surface was not conducive to self-arrests.)

The two other rope teams saw forms at the bottom of the

couloir and started down from the 18,600-foot plateau. A two-man team slipped and fell to the bottom of the couloir; John Morrell broke his wrist in this fall. When they reached the bottom, they found that David Ober had broken his femur and that Dwayne Stranahan had broken his lower leg in the initial fall. The student who caused the fall was uninjured; he had been the major personality problem of the trip, lacking both consideration and judgment.

The two climbers with leg injuries were injected with Demerol. The next day they were dragged down to 15,000 feet in lashed-together pack frames. All three of the injured climbers were evacuated by an Air Force helicopter.

One instructor felt that "they had had plenty" in climbing the South Peak, and had opted out of an attempt on the North Peak because he felt the group was not up to it psychologically. He stated, "Perhaps, given the length of the expedition, the general level of experience, the weather (mediocre) and the superstitious fact that all had gone pretty well so far, perhaps it would have been a wise decision not to push our luck. . . ."

Three years later, on July 11, 1976, the six-man Juneau Denali Expedition reached 18,000 feet on the Pioneer Ridge. The two strongest members of the group, Steve Swenson and Bruce Blume, were well ahead of the other four. They ultimately climbed over the North Peak and descended to Denali Pass. At 5 P.M., Larry Fanning became ill. Joe Ebner radioed out for advice and the Park Service recommended descent. Fanning had acute mountain sickness.

The four climbers decided that the Sourdough Couloir was a better choice than the North Peak or descending by their fixed ropes on the Pioneer Ridge. After failing to catch up with Swenson and Blume, they began their descent on July 12. The couloir was difficult, with six inches of snow over ice, so they fixed ropes to their ice axes. Fanning had broken front points on one crampon. Eight hundred feet down, an ice ax pulled out, and they all fell 1,000 feet down the couloir. Ebner and Richard Rose died during the fall. Bill Joiner was delirious and suspended upside down in the ropes; Fanning had broken his left leg in three places. He tried repeatedly, but unsuccessfully, to right Joiner; he then searched for a radio in Ebner's pack, but couldn't find one. Fanning spent the night without a hat or gloves, while Joiner remained hanging upside down in the ropes.

Seventeen hours after the fall, a Canadian expedition came by. They moved Joiner, then returned and brought Fanning down to their camp at 15,000 feet. The National Park Service radioed a NOLS group who moved the bodies down to the Canadian camp at 15,000 feet and helped to treat Joiner and Fanning.

On July 14, Joiner regained consciousness. However, because of poor communications and the lack of a flight surgeon, the helicopter didn't arrive until 3:45 A.M. on July 15.

Splitting a group up is the most common prelude to accidents on Denali. In the case of the Juneau expedition, Swenson and Blume, the strongest members of the group, would have been a considerable asset to the team during their difficult traverse. The four remaining climbers should have chosen to descend the familiar Pioneer Ridge rather than the unknown Sourdough Couloir. Although they were probably short on hardware, fixing ropes to ice axes is unreliable; ice screws, pickets, flukes or pitons would have been best.

The cost of an Army evacuation of Joiner, Fanning and the two bodies was $11,464.00. The Bicentennial year on Denali was an expensive one for the taxpayer: $82,142.36 was spent on rescue flights. In June of that year, a helicopter pilot, Buddy Woods, charged the National Park Service $8,640.87 for an unprecedented, but bold, evacuation of two women from the very top of North America.

On June 2, 1976, four members of the Denali Women's Expedition slipped and fell 400 feet while descending from the summit on the South Buttress. Jennifer Williams and Paula Kregel suffered minor injuries from hitting their heads on the slope. Williams also hit her head on an ice ax and was unconscious for a short time; Kregel was dizzy and could not walk. Vera Komarkova and Joan Williams left the two at 19,600 feet, climbed over the summit and down Denali Pass to report the accident.

Meanwhile, a hang glider jumped off the summit, crashed and rolled 800 feet down the South Face, which confused matters. Shortly afterwards, a military plane made three air-drops of rope and litters to be used in the two separate evacuations; the airdrops were never found. The hang glider returned to the summit unscathed.

Komarkova's efforts to get a ground team to her injured friends failed; it was too hard to climb over the summit and then carry someone back up and down again at altitude. Ray Genet and pilot Buddy Woods were both extremely anxious to try a helicopter rescue. Finally, when the National Park Service realized there was no other alternative, they gave Woods permission to attempt a rescue. Woods dropped Genet off at 20,100 feet, literally on the summit, and Genet descended to Williams and Kregel. He found that their injuries were not as serious as originally estimated by Komarkova. He assisted Williams down a short distance, where Woods boldly hovered on the edge of a crevasse, and loaded her into the helicopter. Genet and a climber who had been dropped off with him moved Kregel down to a plateau at 18,700 feet, northeast of the summit; Woods then picked up both Kregel and the other climber. After

121

transferring Kregel to an airplane on the Kahiltna Glacier, Woods returned for Genet.

No helicopter had ever landed that high on Denali before. (In 1980, Mike Covington had evacuated a client with HAPE from the same spot because a helicopter rescue was not feasible.) Without Woods, Genet, the third rescuer and a bit of luck, the two climbers would have died.

The Bicentennial year attracted a record number of climbers who were involved in a disproportionately high number of rescues. Climbers knew that they could call for a helicopter if they were in trouble and that rescues were seldom, if ever, denied. It is more than likely that the availability of helicopters on Denali prompted both brash climbing attitudes and a lack of initiative in self-evacuation; both of these can be fatal in more isolated areas such as the Cordillera Blanca in Peru or the Himalaya.

The next year, 1977, a veteran climber fell and broke his ankle on a hard route on Mount Hunter, Denali's neighbor. The climber's two companions lowered him down 4,000 feet of steep ice and helped him into an airplane at the landing strip. They never considered a helicopter winch evacuation, nor did they carry a radio. The two remaining climbers, Mike Kennedy and George Lowe, finished the new route on Mount Hunter and then climbed a new route on nearby Mount Foraker. They were accomplished climbers, setting a stylish example that few injured parties on Denali chose to repeat. Many inexperienced climbers are drawn to Denali because of its reputation; once injured, however, they lack the skill to perform a self-evacuation.

On May 19, 1983, a team left their 16,600-foot camp on the Wickersham Wall for the north summit. In raw weather at 18,600 feet, Evelyn Lees and Rick Wyatt lashed their ice axes on their packs and turned back while their partners continued to the top. Shortly afterward, Lees slipped on 30-degree snow and, being unroped and lacking an ax to self-arrest with, she slid 800 feet, until the slope flattened out near camp.

During the fall, Lees had broken her right ulna and cracked her pelvis. Wyatt helped her back to camp.

After a rest day, the team carried Lees' pack and lowered her down the steeper sections. On May 21, Dr. Peter Hackett examined her at the 14,300-foot medical camp and suspected a fracture of the hip. Although he requested a helicopter evacuation, stormy weather prevented it.

Meanwhile, the following afternoon, while descending below windpack and ice below Denali Pass, Niklaus Lotscher slipped and bowled over his partner, Bill Baker. Although he was able to stop after several attempts at self-arresting, Lotscher fell 1,000 feet. Baker descended and found his partner conscious, but with facial cuts, a broken wrist and possible cervical injuries (he complained of neck pain).

Brian Okonek, a mountain guide, saw the fall and arrived within 40 minutes to help evacuate Lotscher. They called the Talkeetna Ranger Station for a helicopter pickup, and lowered Lotscher to a suitable landing spot.

At 9 P.M., I watched beads of sweat run down the pilot's (Jim Porter's) forehead as we hovered toward Lotscher at 17,000 feet; 22 years earlier a pilot and rescuer were caught here in a downdraft and killed. Suddenly the Alouette III plummeted like a broken elevator as it was pulled toward the glacier in a downdraft. Porter gave it full power and steered for a huge, wide crevasse as we shot past rescuers and victim. We were forced down into the hole at over 90 mph, then shot out the end into 8,000 feet of space.

Instead of trying again, we circled to 14,300 feet on the West

Buttress to evacuate Lees and another frostbitten climber, Claudia Berryman. The light faded as we autorotated in. Hackett windvaned his arms to mark the landing site, but we lost sight of him in the blizzard created by the rotor. Porter shouted to open the door and tell him how close we were. Just as I yelled, "I can't see . . . ," we slammed against the snow, rocked forward, and Porter trimmed the power. Spindrift settled on our laps.

I jumped out and escorted Lees and Berryman to the chopper. We took off immediately, but were forced to climb to 18,000 feet, above the cloud layer that had blown in. Meanwhile, the two victims chatted away in the back seat as if it were a taxi ride. After ten minutes, figuring that we had passed all the peaks, we descended blind into the clouds. Then the low-fuel buzzer wailed and flashed red. Ten minutes of fuel remained and we were 30 minutes from Talkeetna; the fuel had burned off while flying up high. Nor did we know where we were.

After five minutes of blind cloud flying, we finally ducked under the clouds, and the brown terminus of the Ruth Glacier popped into view—we had skipped over the granite walls of the gorge. We flew toward the headlights of a car on the highway, several miles away, and landed on an asphalt pullout. As Porter radioed for a plane to come rescue the rescuers with some helicopter fuel, I ran out onto the highway, pulled open some flares and stopped most of the traffic. Doug Geeting's Supercub split the night and landed on the double yellow line.

We poured 20 gallons of fuel into the Alouette III; then Geeting vaulted from his plane as a semi-truck driver roared into the pullout, slammed on his brakes and skidded to within several feet of Geeting's wing.

From Talkeetna, Lees and Berryman flew to Anchorage in another plane. On the drive from the airport to the hospital,

Lowering Niklaus Lotscher after his fall from Denali. *Brian Okonek*

they convinced their taxi driver to stop at a fast-food restaurant for dinner—the Anchorage Daily News reported this the next day. They were both released with minor frostbite and a bruised hip. And no one thanked Porter, Geeting, or me.

Several days later, during the next window in the storm, Porter picked up Lotscher from 17,000 feet (he turned out to have no cervical injuries). The taxpayer picked up the $12,214 bill.

In retrospect, the amount of risk, time and money that rescuers (and taxpayers) expended upon these two climbing falls is not unusual. Certainly, Lees could have stopped her fall if she were carrying an ice ax, while Lotscher might well have stopped his fall if he had been as practiced in self-arrest as his partner.

Three weeks later, I heard two Japanese climbers on the West Buttress radio for help. Nobuyoshi Chiba and Masato Watanabe had fallen while descending from the summit directly from 19,200 feet, instead of coming down to Denali Pass. Within hours of the call, Brian Okonek, Peter Hackett, Jeff Rhoades, Ed Anderson and I left the 17,200-foot camp at 10:30 P.M. with hot drinks, medical supplies and rescue rope. We reached the pair at midnight.

Anderson and Rhoades immediately walked Watanabe down, while Hackett splinted Chiba's broken leg. We then placed him inside a sleeping bag and a haul sack, and spent the rest of the evening lowering him back down to 17,200 feet. Two days later, two other volunteers helped me lower Chiba down the final 3,000 feet to the medical camp. On June 13, Lowell Thomas evacuated Chiba from the 14,300-foot camp in his Helio–Courier airplane.

The team's leader, Mikio Yamakami, had been evacuated nearly a week earlier with HAPE, which probably eroded the

Lowering Chiba down rescue gully, 1983. *JONATHAN WATERMAN*

already inexperienced team's judgment. The two climbers not only had no business on this steep short cut to the summit, but all the rescuers expressed dismay that the uninjured Watanabe took no initiative in evacuating the injured Chiba. Without relatively mild weather (20 degrees below zero) and rescuers, both Chiba and Watanabe would probably have died in their complacent bivouac.

In 1987, the Messner Couloir was the site of two serious climbing falls. At 6:20 A.M. on June 7, Thomas Bohanon left his 16,600-foot camp in the Couloir and began plugging up the deep snow towards the 19,400-foot plateau; from here, he continued walking to the summit. During his descent back down the Couloir, he tripped when a strap dangling from his pack caught his crampon. As he couldn't fix the problem, he continued down. At 5 P.M. his crampon caught on the strap again; this time he fell forward, plunging a terrifying 1,500 feet, until he came to rest 900 feet below his camp.

Miraculously, people at the medical camp below witnessed his fall, and within two hours, ten men reached Bohanon. He was unable to walk, so he was lowered five rope lengths, then dragged across the plateau to the medical camp. Within four hours of his fall, he was helicoptered out to Humana Hospital in Anchorage and diagnosed as having an avulsion fracture of his hip.

A month later, Polish climbers Piotr Jankowiak and Jacek Jezierski summited, then returned to their 18,900-foot camp in the Messner Couloir. At 11:30 P.M. on July 3, instead of crossing over to the West Buttress route, they moved into another 30- to 40-degree couloir and began sliding down on their rear ends while carrying full packs. Suddenly, Jankowiak accelerated, lost control and plummeted 2,600 feet; his shocked partner crossed over to the West Buttress route and ran down to

14,300 feet to find two of his countrymen. At 3:20 A.M., they located Jankowiak at 14,700 feet, dead from his pounding against the rock cliffs in the couloir.

Both Bohanon and Jankowiak chose to go up and down the Messner Couloir. In 1976, however, Reinhold Messner, instead of descending the couloir, chose the simple and safe descent down the West Buttress. In Bohanon's case, it was fortunate that people saw his fall; soloing, of course, can incur a premium penalty. And the Polish climbers' sitting glissade with full packs and crampons is not recommended under the best of conditions, particularly when one is unfamiliar with the couloir's runout. Jankowiak was the eighteenth climber to die in a climbing fall on Denali.

To date, 26 climbers have died in climbing falls—the most common accident on the mountain. Prevention of hypothermia and altitude sickness, and avoidance of the summit during mediocre weather could reduce the likelihood of a fall. Proper ice-ax training could also help to arrest slides. But, when all preventive measures fail, climbers must learn how to evacuate themselves to a lower elevation.

SUMMARY: CLIMBING FALLS

DATE	NAME	ROUTE & ELEVATION OF INCIDENT	COMMENTS
4/29/70	LUZ SMITH	W RIB 13000	SLIPPED NOT ATTACHED TO FIXED LINE
6/4/72	WITTE	W BUTTRESS 18000	SNOW GAVE WAY
6/29/72	WATANABE TOYAMA YAJIMA	W RIB 18000	FELL 1500-2500 FEET WHILE DESCENDING
5/29/73	BROWN	W BUTTRESS 17500	ALTITUDE SICKNESS, GROUP SELF-ARREST FAILED
7/13/73	OBER MORRELL STRANAHAN	HARPER GLACIER 18800	FELL 800 FEET
5/27/74	OKADO	CASSIN 12200	FIXED ROPE BROKE ON RAPPEL, FELL 800 FEET
6/2/76	WILLIAMS KREGEL	S BUTTRESS 19600	FELL 400 FEET
7/12/76	EBNER ROSE FANNING JOINER	PIONEER RIDGE 16900	PARTY SEPARATED, ICE AX ANCHOR FAILED
7/21/76	SCHMIDT	W BUTTRESS 18800	NO ICE AX, UNROPED, FELL 1000 FEET
5/22/79	CURRENS	S BUTTRESS 10000	240-FOOT LEADER FALL
5/29/79	KO LEE PARK	W RIB 18000	SLIP, SELF-ARREST FAILED

130

HOW EVACUATED	RESULT	RESCUED BY	GOVERNMENT COST
BURIED ON MOUNTAIN	2 DEATHS		NONE
HELICOPTER	BROKEN LEG	*	$2000
AIRPLANE	3 DEATHS	SHELDON	$4000
HELICOPTER	CONCUSSION	*	$1000
HELICOPTER	BROKEN FEMUR BROKEN LEG BROKEN WRIST	AIR FORCE	$1200
HELICOPTER	DEATH	ANCHORAGE HELICOPTER SERVICE	$1250
HELICOPTER	MINOR INJURIES	WOODS AIR SERVICE	$8640.87
HELICOPTER	2 DEATHS	ARMY	$11464
LEFT ON MOUNTAIN	DEATH		$5644
HELICOPTER	BROKEN FEMUR	AKLAND HELICOPTER SERVICE	$3268.07
HELICOPTER	2 DEATHS, FROSTBITE	ARMY	*

*INDICATES INFORMATION NOT AVAILABLE
**IN 1982, THE ARMY BILLED THE NPS $67,000 FOR ALL RESCUE OPERATIONS.

SUMMARY: CLIMBING FALLS

DATE	NAME	ROUTE & ELEVATION OF INCIDENT	COMMENTS
5/11/80	HERRMAN	W BUTTRESS 18000	UNROPED
5/16/82	MCDANIEL	W BUTTRESS 17500	ROPED FALL
5/26/82	FROHN	W BUTTRESS 18000	UNROPED, FELL 500 FEET
6/4/82	KANDA IDA	W RIB 18800	FELL 2000 FEET WHILE DESCENDING
5/17/89	CHRIS MASSEY JOHN LANG JULIAN DIXON	W RIB 18300	CLIMBING IN STORM, NO PROTECTION
5/12/85	MARC WILLIAMS	W RIB 16000	SLIPPED IN OVERBOOTS
5/3/87	STAN DARKE	W RIB 14800	CLIMBING UNROPED
6/9/90	MICHAEL KOSHUTA STUART JONES	W RIB 15800	FELL WHILE TRAVERSING OFF CASSIN
5/19/83	EVELYN LEES	WICKERSHAM WALL 18000	ICE AX CARRIED ON PACK
5/22/83	NIKLAUS LOTSCHER	W BUTTRESS 18000	INABILITY TO SELF ARREST
6/10/83	NOBUYOSHI CHIBA	W BUTTRESS 19200	INAPPROPRIATE ROUTE SELECTION
6/7/87	THOMAS BOHANON	MESSNER COULOIR 17000	STRAP CAUGHT CRAMPONS
7/3/87	PIOTR JANKOWIAK	MESSNER COULOIR 18800	FELL WHILE GLISSADING

HOW EVACUATED	RESULT	RESCUED BY	GOVERNMENT COST
HELICOPTER	DEATH	AKLAND HELICOPTER SERVICE	$3268.07
HELICOPTER	BROKEN ANKLE	ARMY	**
HELICOPTER	COMPRESSION FRACTURE: VERTEBRAE	ARMY	**
HELICOPTER	HEAD INJURIES, FROSTBITE	ARMY	**
HELICOPTER	3 DEATHS	NPS, SOLOY HELICOPTER	$4856
HELICOPTER	DEATH	MUGS STUMP, MARTY SCHMIDT, ERA HELICOPTER	$1456
HELICOPTER WINCH	COMA	NPS, US ARMY	$33754
LEFT ON MOUNTAIN	2 DEATHS	NPS	$4606
SELF/HELICOPTER	BROKEN ULNA	JIM PORTER, EVERGREEN HELICOPTERS	(SEE LOTSCHER)
HELICOPTER	BROKEN WRIST	BRIAN OKONEK, JIM PORTER EVERGREEN	$12214
AIRPLANE	BROKEN LEG	NPS, BRIAN OKONEK, PETER HACKETT	NO COST
HELICOPTER	AVULSION FRACTURE OF HIP	ERA HELICOPTERS	$6594
SLED/AIRPLANE	DEATH	TALKEETNA AIR TAXI	$655

*INDICATES INFORMATION NOT AVAILABLE
**IN 1982, THE ARMY BILLED THE NPS $67,000 FOR ALL RESCUE OPERATIONS.

C H A P T E R

C r e v a s s e   F a l l s

Getting Ken out was an epic
struggle. He is lucky to be alive
and but for his strength and
toughness probably would not be.

Ian Wade

Poor glacier-travel technique, such as slack rope or soloing, causes most serious crevasse accidents on Denali. Bad falls have occurred after rest stops when the lead climber is not belayed out of the rest area, when climbers have stepped beyond probed campsites, or when climbers have tied in too closely to one another. Worst of all, unroped glacier travel has resulted in at least five deaths (and two unconfirmed disappearances).

In 1932, the obstinate, yet very experienced, Allen Carpé was snowshoeing down the Muldrow Glacier unroped. Both he and his companion, Theodore Koven, died after falling into a crevasse. From the evidence, it appears that Koven had gone back up the glacier on skis to try and rescue Carpé from a crevasse, and that he eventually fell into it himself.

A National Park Service Patrol dragged Koven's body (they could not find Carpé's) down the Muldrow, tied to their sled with a climbing rope. One ropeless ranger, Grant Pearson, almost became the third fatality when he fell into a crevasse and had to be rescued. Fortunately his injuries were slight.

In February 1967, Jacques Batkin, an experienced French climber who had cut his teeth on the French Ridge of Mount Huntington a few years earlier, died in a crevasse fall a mile from Kahiltna base camp at 7,000 feet; he was unroped. Although another member of the team had fallen into the same crevasse the day before, the crevasse was left unwanded.

Apparently, Batkin was an irrepressible individual who preferred travelling alone. His fall could probably have been prevented if he had been aware of the earlier fall. Communication about dangers is important, as there are many other strong, individualistic climbers like Batkin who solo Denali's glaciers.

In June 1971, four National Outdoor Leadership School climbers arrived at 9,300 feet on the Muldrow Glacier. They remained roped while they marked out a circle and probed for crevasses. Then Dr. Bob Bullard took off his snowshoes, untied himself from the rope and stepped outside of the circle to urinate. He broke through a crevasse, grabbed the middle of a rope that was lying at his feet and slid down the rope. Randy Cerf held one end of the rope while another teammate dived unsuccessfully for the other. Although it appeared that Bullard would be held by Cerf, the rope suddenly went slack when Bullard could no longer hold on.

He fell 130 feet to his death at the bottom of the crevasse. Gary Ullin, an experienced climber with another party, rappelled down into the crevasse and tied a rope to the body. It was then hauled up and dragged down to 7,300 feet. On July 2, Don Sheldon flew the body out.

The team used good judgment in probing their campsite. However, despite the strength of the party or someone's intuition about hidden crevasses, even the safest of techniques can be undone by a moment's inattention.

In April 1976, during their approach to the Cassin Ridge, a

Ken Jern being assisted after his crevasse extrication in 1976.
IAN WADE

six-man party stopped for a rest at 10,300 feet on the East Fork of the Kahiltna. Ian Wade and Ray Smutek started off; ten minutes later, Ken Jern followed in their tracks. After half a rope length, he broke through a crevasse bridge and fell 70 feet to the bottom, landing on his buttocks. Like many climbers leaving rest stops, he was not belayed; in part, this was because Wade and Smutek had passed over the same area without incident. The party had been worried about crevasses earlier in the day, during an icefall, but had relaxed their guard in the rest area because it was flat and they could not see any surface sinking that would indicate crevasses.

Wade rappelled down into the crevasse and dug Jern out from under some ice blocks which had fallen onto him. It took three hours to haul him out; he was unconscious and extremely hypothermic. The night of April 11, he was delirious.

They nursed Jern for the next three days. Eventually his condition began to improve, and he was able to walk alone, but with difficulty. They had sent two climbers out to the landing strip, but the radio was not there yet; they could not use their own CB radio because they were not up high enough. Finally, on April 17, a bush pilot was notified at the landing strip and Jern was evacuated the following day.

One means of reducing the severity of crevasse falls would be to consistently belay out of rest stops, regardless of the interpretation of the terrain. There are many good climbers who have overlooked similar small, but important, aspects of glacier-travel technique and paid dearly for their carelessness.

Two weeks after Jern was evacuated, a party on the Muldrow Glacier split up when one of their sleeping bags blew away at 10,700 feet; two of the climbers started down. At 7,000 feet, when Andrew Stepniewski was passing Carl Ellingsen, he broke

John Thackray crossing a crevasse in the Northeast Fork of Kahiltna Glacier. *JONATHAN WATERMAN*

through a crevasse bridge and fell 60 feet to the bottom. At the time, there was a great deal of slack in the rope.

Ellingsen got Stepniewski out with help from another party. He was unconscious for 15 minutes, then became delirious. He suffered a minor concussion, but was able to walk out several days later.

Many people might describe this incident as a run of bad luck. Another interpretation is that the pair were actually very *lucky* to have made so many mistakes with only minor consequences. Equipment as invaluable as a sleeping bag should be tied down, and slack in the rope negates the inherent advantages of roped travel. The two were also very fortunate that another party was nearby to assist in removing Stepniewski from the crevasse.

On March 13, 1982, a British climber, Roger Mear, roped up with a Spaniard he did not know and started up the Kahiltna Glacier to retrieve a cache of gear. As Mike Young and I could not help because our feet were frostbitten, we remained in a snow cave at the 7,000-foot landing strip. Because of the language barrier, Mear and the Spaniard could not communicate with one another. The Spanish climber moved behind Mear, leaving a lot of slack in the rope. It is possible that he was unfamiliar with Denali's hidden crevasses and with proper glacier-travel techniques. Two miles out from base camp, Mear broke through a crevasse bridge and fell 30 feet to the bottom because of the slack in the rope. He severed some ligaments in his knee, but was able to jumar out. The Spaniard left Mear in order to get help. Meanwhile, Mear tied his skis together and pushed himself a mile down the Glacier. Here he met the three Spanish climbers, who dragged him back to the landing strip on a sled. We all waited three more days for our overdue bush pilot to evacuate us from the landing strip.

Mear's accident illustrates the importance of having good communication and ropemates who have climbed together before.

In mid-April 1981, John Mallon Waterman set out alone up the Northwest Fork of the Ruth Glacier to solo a new route on the East Buttress. One party observed that his tracks made a beeline through a heavily crevassed area. Another party saw his snowshoe tracks and described them as a "crazy route in and out of slots [crevasses]." An old campsite was found at 7,200 feet on the glacier but, despite extensive air and ground searches, no further trace of Waterman was ever found. Waterman had soloed Mount Hunter in 1978; an incredible 148-day climb. His father, Guy Waterman, commented that Johnny knew the intricacies of the Alaska Range so well, that his disappearance was no accident. Both Carpé and Batkin resembled Waterman, with their considerable experience on Alaskan glaciers, and being individualists who felt comfortable alone and unroped.

One could speculate that such personality traits, combined with a relaxation of attention to dangers, caused their crevasse deaths. Less experienced, team-oriented climbers who rope in have a better chance of surviving. It is also interesting to note that all three of these climbers wore snowshoes, which are not as safe in crevassed areas as skis.

For the ensuing decade, solo crevasse falls continued. In May 1983, soloist Rick Morlock snowshoed out from the 11,000-foot West Buttress camp with a 60-pound pack. Because of snowy, whiteout conditions, Morlock ventured off the trail. Several hundred feet above camp, he fell 20 feet into a crevasse, landed on a snow bridge and was knocked unconscious. Fortunately, he was able to climb out two hours later.

He sustained a mild concussion, descended the route and

A dangerous technique: unroped and improperly dressed on the
Kahiltna Glacier. *JONATHAN WATERMAN*

flew out to Talkeetna two days later. The Park Rangers had already warned Morlock about glacier soloing, but as often happens, they are powerless to stop anyone from foolhardy endeavors.

The next year, on June 6, in similar poor visibility conditions, just below where Morlock fell, a guided Swiss party finished shuttling loads up the glacier. Peter Nadler, a seasoned European guide, started skiing back down off the trail. Just before coming to a stop, two clients observed Nadler break into a crevasse as the bridge crumbled away beneath him.

The crevasse was six feet wide at the top, but significantly overhung beneath its lip. The rest of the party shouted down, but there was no answer. As the party had no ropes, two members started back up to find help.

Finally, some Austrians came to their assistance. Once they were lowered down, they found the overhanging lip of the crevasse quite dangerous. After considerable difficulty, more than six hours after Nadler had fallen into the crevasse, they finally uncovered his body. Because of the depth of the crevasse and its overhanging lip, Nadler's body was abandoned.

This particular accident is common among European climbers on Denali, who often travel unroped, perhaps lulled into complacency because of their experiences on safer, dry glaciers in the Alps. Furthermore, it is quite difficult to ski roped, and skiing off the trail, on a day with poor visibility, is an invitation to a crevasse fall. Finally, if the team had carried a rope, let alone tied into one, they might either have been able to prevent Nadler's fall, or rescue him.

On June 17, 1987, Brian Hoover flew into the 7,000-foot landing strip. The Park Rangers informed me that he intended to solo the Cassin Ridge, but had little experience in alpinism; I strolled over to his camp for a chat. Hoover seemed quite open

145

Crossing a crevasse on the Muldrow Glacier. *JONATHAN WATERMAN*

to suggestion, so I told him that soloing up the Northeast Fork of the Kahiltna to the base of the Cassin was deadly business, and that he might not come back.

Instead, I suggested that, if he had to solo, he should climb the West Buttress, stay on the trail, get acclimatized and leave a cache up high. Then, provided he still wanted to do the Cassin Ridge, he should find someone to rope up with for the dangerous, crevassed terrain on the approach.

Two weeks later, Hoover reached the summit, via the upper West Rib route, and descended back to 14,300 feet on the West Buttress. He asked several parties for details about the Cassin. The last climbers to see him alive, on July 5, tried to deter him, or at least get him to take a rope. Hoover seemed unaware of the difficulties of the route—certainly he had never approached anything of its magnitude before.

When his due-out date passed on July 20, Doug Geeting flew over the Cassin and looked for him. Aerial searches continued for the next week. Although some tracks were seen in the upper Northeast Fork, Hoover's body was never recovered; $14,584 was expended in aerial searches. In all likelihood, he fell into a crevasse or was buried in one of the enormous avalanches that frequently blanket the area.

Even seasoned alpinists who have soloed the Cassin Ridge have arranged to rope up with another party for the crevassed approach. Hoover, however, had not served an apprenticeship that would give him the proper judgment and skills for the dangers and difficulties of such a route. It is also important to remember that after July, the glaciers soften considerably. This increases the likelihood of falling into crevasses, making solo trips more reckless, even on the well-traveled West Buttress.

On May 8, 1981, Jim Wickwire and Chris Kerrebrock, two strong, experienced climbers, were involved in a horrible accident on Denali. They were walking together on a short, 20-foot rope, at 6,700 feet on the Peters Glacier, en route to the Wickersham Wall. They were both attached by nylon webbing to one large sled that was between them. Although Kerrebrock had previously fallen thigh deep into several crevasses, they had presented no real problem because the two were roped together. Just before the accident, they had come onto an area of glacier which seemed safe because they could not see any sagging snow bridges or crevasses (Jern's party had made the same observation). Suddenly Kerrebrock fell into a hidden crevasse and Wickwire was pulled through the air; he landed on top of both the sled and Kerrebrock, 25 feet down in a narrow crevasse.

Kerrebrock was wedged in very tightly and, despite hours of intense effort, Wickwire could not free him. First he tried pulling Kerrrebrock out from outside the crevasse; then he tried from the inside, by stepping into a sling-pulley. He also tried to chop Kerrebrock out and, in futility, attempted to cut Kerrebrock's pack off with an ice hammer. Wickwire finally gave up. As he had broken his shoulder in the initial fall, he was unable to use his arms anymore.

Kerrebrock died from hypothermia about three hours later. So that others could learn what had happened to them, Kerrebrock had told Wickwire not to solo up the glacier and meet a similar fate. Because he was in a walled-in area and their CB radio could only transmit line-of-sight, Wickwire waited five days for a plane to fly over. On the sixth day, he slowly picked his way up the Peters Glacier, probing each step of the way to locate other crevasses. He was finally picked up by glacier pilot Doug Geeting in a tricky landing near Kahiltna Pass.

Although using a short rope was convenient for dragging the sled, and seemed safe initially, a longer rope would have had greater stretch and absorption, and could have prevented Wick-

A body recovery from a crevasse. *SCOTT GILL*

A dangerous technique: unroped hauling on the Kahiltna Glacier
JONATHAN WATERMAN

wire from being pulled into the crevasse on top of Kerrebrock. Also two sleds, instead of one heavy sled pulled between the climbers, might have proved a safer means of transport.

Sleds, although helpful for transporting gear, can be dangerous during a crevasse fall. For instance, on May 20, 1983, just a few miles from the 7,000-foot landing strip, Dale Van Dalsem stepped over a small crevasse. He felt it was too obvious to bother warning his wife, Jacqueline. Shortly afterward, Jacqueline fell about 12 feet into the crevasse. A 70-pound sled was tied into her waist harness.

Two minutes after the fall, another team member was belayed to the edge of the crevasse and heard Van Dalsem mutter, "Help me." Five minutes later, the team set up a "z" pulley system and began hauling Van Dalsem up. No one went into the crevasse to help her and no further voice contact was made.

While being hauled up, her body jammed on the crevasse lip. Someone then went down, took off her pack, cut off the sled, and shoveled away the lip. They started hauling again, but her harness gave way and she fell another 30 feet back into the crevasse.

Finally, climbers from another party went down into the crevasse and guided Van Dalsem over the lip as she was hauled up. The 16-member team had taken two hours to get Van Dalsem out. Once she was on the glacier, they initiated CPR, but she never responded. Her body was sledded back to the landing strip and flown out to Talkeetna on May 21.

This incident shows how difficult it can be for even a large party to perform a crevasse rescue. Ideally, in such situations, traveling in the early hours of the morning, when crevasse bridges are frozen, particularly in the warmer months of the summer, is highly recommended. In the event of a fall, a climber should descend into the crevasse immediately to provide first aid to the victim and help with the extrication. Finally, although it is cumbersome to tie sleds and packs to a climbing rope, the technique is recommended—the autopsy implies that the heavy sled hanging from Van Dalsem killed her.

Careful attention to every detail of glacier travel is essential in order to prevent crevasse falls. Climbers should be tied in at least 50 feet apart (farther apart if there are only two climbers on a rope), and ropes should be kept taut or belayed before and after stops. Even if a glacier seems safe, treating it casually has led to many accidents. Probe for crevasses at every camp or rest area. Practice jumaring, and using the z pulley and other crevasse rescue systems before you start up the glacier. Avoid travel in the hottest part of the day below 10,000 feet when crevasse snow bridges are soft. And remember that a crevasse is like an instant deep freeze; regardless of the surface temperature of the glacier, hypothermia will be an issue for any scantily clad crevasse-fall victim.

Five climbers have died on Denali during roped falls into crevasses. And seven more have died while enjoying the addictive freedom and speed of soloing. Unroped travel remains popular, particularly on the crowded Kahiltna Glacier (where most of the crevasse falls occur). If this trend continues, more climbers will die inside a cold, dark hole before they even begin their climb of the mountain.

SUMMARY: CREVASSE FALLS

DATE	NAME	ROUTE & ELEVATION OF INCIDENT	COMMENTS
6/24/71	BULLARD	MULDROW 9300	UNROPED, STEPPED OUT OF PROBED AREA
4/11/76	JERN	E FORK KAHILTNA 7000	NOT BELAYED OUT OF REST AREA
4/19/81	WATERMAN	NW FORK RUTH 7200+	DISAPPEARED, PROBABLE CREVASSE FALL
5/1/76	STEPNIEWSKI	MULDROW 7000	PASSING WITH SLACK IN ROPE
5/8/81	KERREBROCK WICKWIRE	PETERS GLACIER 6700	SHORT ROPE
3/13/82	MEAR	W BUTTRESS 7000	LANGUAGE BARRIER, SLACK ROPE
5/22/83	RICK MORLOCK	W BUTTRESS 11300	SOLOING
6/6/84	PETER NADLER	W BUTTRESS 10500	SKIING UNROPED
JULY 1987	BRIAN HOOVER	UNKNOWN	INEXPERIENCED SOLOIST
5/20/83	JACQUELINE VAN DALSEM	W BUTTRESS 7400	HEAVY SLED AND PACK

156

HOW EVACUATED	RESULT	RESCUED BY	GOVERNMENT COST
SLED, AIRPLANE	DEATH	*	$300
HELICOPTER	2 CRUSHED VERTEBRAE, BROKEN ARM, MINOR FROSTBITE ON HAND	INTERNATIONAL AIR TAXI	$3453.07
BODY NEVER RECOVERED	DEATH	NPS	$6211.12
ON FOOT	MINOR CONCUSSION		NONE
HELICOPTER ON FOOT, PLANE	DEATH BROKEN SHOULDER	NPS	$5203.25
SLED	SEVERED LIGAMENTS		NONE
ON FOOT	MILD CONCUSSION	SELF	NONE
LEFT IN CREVASSE	DEATH		NONE
	NEVER RECOVERED		$14584
OWN PARTY	DEATH	OWN PARTY	$2422

*INDICATES INFORMATION NOT AVAILABLE

CHAPTER SEVEN

Avalanches

*When Big Bertha let loose
the first thing I realized was the
horrible nature of the sound.
It was an awesome event and one
that left me shaken, almost limp,
because the power was so evident.*

Alan Danson
SOUTH BUTTRESS, 1982

Four Canadian and American climbers disappeared in July 1980 during an attempt on the Cassin Ridge route. A year later, three Japanese climbers vanished while attempting the American Direct route on the South Face. Although no trace of any of the seven climbers was ever found, it is supposed that they were buried and killed in avalanches.

Although avalanches comprise only a small percent of the serious accidents on Denali, they are usually deadly, particularly on some of the steeper routes or approaches to the South Face. Snow and ice avalanches are little different from storms, crevasses and rockfall—all are objective dangers that can be minimized by route selection and, in part, by luck.

Rod Newcomb, president of the American Avalanche Institute, describes his avalanche encounter:

> In the spring of 1963 Peter Lev and I were on the first ascent
> of the East Buttress of Denali. Other members of the expedi-

tion were Al, Jed, Fred and Warren. The avalanche lore of the climbers was limited. Only two, Warren and I, had been on a major expedition to a big mountain before. All the climbers had some skiing experience, but no practice with avalanche forecasting and control. Our knowledge of stability evaluation came primarily from the 1961 edition of *The ABC of Avalanche Safety*. We had an expedition copy with us.

On May 1, Peter and I began the climbing on the route and climbed the first difficult section immediately above base camp. This section became known as the Bulge and, as Jed describes it, "The route is over a 60-degree snow and sugar ice slope with occasional open and hidden crevasses." Pete and I fixed this section with 5/16-inch manila rope. Fred and Jed followed with loads to be cached and eventually carried higher to Camp 1.

My diary of May 1 does not mention anything about dangerous snow conditions, but I remember noting the harder snow underlain by loose granular snow. Peter's diary reads for May 1, "Up at 4 A.M.—fantastic colors and cold and clear. Rod, Jed, Fred and myself leave at 5 A.M. for the Buttress and the first difficult pitch. I get the difficult lead. It is very steep, rotten ice overlain by rotten snow, then a foot thick snow slab. I am uncertain and very slow. I take most of the morning for the 150-foot lead. At the top we fix manila line and bring loads up." Pete must have been impressed by the snow conditions to note them in his diary. It was a difficult pitch since it was hard to get firm footing after breading through the slab into the loose snow beneath. Pete may have been worried about an avalanche.

After we climbed the Bulge, I dismissed any thought of an avalanche on that portion of the route. Jed and Fred followed us and we all descended that same afternoon.

The next day (May 2) continued to be clear. I was climbing alone attached only to the fixed rope and had climbed the

Bulge and was waiting for Pete and Jed who were a few minutes behind me. Peter's diary reads, "Bright and clear— up at 3 A.M., off by 4 A.M. Warren and Al go ahead to recon. Pass the Bulge quickly. We find this pitch easy climbing compared to yesterday—it is hard surface—but as I reach the point of greatest convexity the slab breaks—avalanche. The fixed line holds Jed and me as snow sweeps over us. High up dangerous warm slopes. Argument with Warren. High ice avalanche breaks off southeast spur and sweeps over base camp and Fred (who remained behind) is okay, but what a fright. Eight huge sympathetic avalanches started."

I did not hear nor could I see the avalanche from where I was waiting. After I thought they should have arrived at the top of the Bulge, I started to descend when they topped the Bulge and reported the avalanche. It was estimated to be 200 feet long and 300 feet across, with a two-foot fracture.

Several things deserve comment. First, before the avalanche on the Bulge, a total of seven ascents and four descents were made in a period of 24 hours. The party that triggered the avalanche was on the eighth and ninth ascents.

Secondly, the avalanche on the Bulge was only a few hours before the large avalanches that occurred around the rim of the southeast fork of the Ruth Glacier. It was very apparent that these were the first warm days of spring with air temperatures near freezing during the heat of the day.

Thirdly, it is interesting to note that Peter mentions an argument with Warren. The argument was about the stability of the snow on the route above the bulge. Warren was killed on the Matterhorn in a climbing accident. I have learned that when members of a party differ in their stability evaluation, it is wise to bow to the judgment of the most conservative member. Some members of the party may know more about snow and may have more experience but they may be overlooking something that someone else has spotted or feels. All

Avalanche seen from the East Buttress. *JED WILLIAMSON*

too often, a backcountry traveler is on some ego trip and tries to cross a slope which, if he could clear his mind and reflect on the stability of the slope, he would back off.

In 1978, Joseph Carmichael and Al Fons Aaporta were climbing the lower West Rib couloir immediately after a three-day storm. At the top of the couloir, they were caught in an avalanche and carried 1,500 feet to the bottom. It would appear that they triggered the avalanche themselves as the slope was probably heavily loaded with snow after the storm.

Carmichael dug both himself and Aaporta out of the avalanche. He then put Aaporta, who had a compound ankle fracture and an injured thigh, into a sleeping bag. The next morning, he skied out of the heavily crevassed and avalanche-prone Northeast Fork of the Kahiltna with a broken and sprained ankle. After six miles, he met another party which signalled a passing plane to land. Carmichael was evacuated on the spot and Aaporta was picked up by a helicopter that afternoon.

In May 1981, Mike Covington had a close call within 24 hours after a snowstorm on the West Rib. A large, spontaneous powder avalanche ran down the couloir and would have swept him off his feet if he had not been attached to a fixed line.

In May 1982, a 100-foot-wide, six-inch-deep avalanche broke off beneath the weight of a solo climber, and swept down from 13,300 feet to the bottom of the 40- to 50-degree lower West Rib couloir. One of four Swiss climbers in the couloir was swept 700 feet to the bottom, but was uninjured.

The area above the West Rib couloir is a concave, snow deposition zone. The slope angle is 10 to 35 degrees, which allows snow to accumulate rather than sliding off. If climbers could avoid this and other similar deposition zones on the mountain for at least 24 hours after a storm, the snow would settle and be a lot safer to travel on. Unfortunately, because of the surplus of bad weather on Denali, climbers are sometimes forced to travel as soon as the storm clears.

In the crowded European Alps, numerous accidents have occurred in which climbers knock rocks, cornices, avalanches and even themselves onto parties below. As the traffic on Denali increases, one more objective danger will have to be added to the list: climbers above.

In June 1982, a storm-loaded slope broke off beneath Jonathan Chester, Ben Read and Anne Fletcher as they descended to the East Fork of the Kahiltna from the West Fork of the Ruth Glacier. The group had waited out a two-day storm that had dropped two to three feet of snow and was accompanied by high winds.

Chester had lived through a devastating avalanche in the Himalaya, and all of them were aware of the avalanche potential on the East Fork; however, lack of food dictated descent. They were skiing, roped, on a 25-degree slope with Read first, followed by Fletcher and Chester. Read made a kick turn that triggered a slab avalanche between Chester and Fletcher and carried all three of them down 200 feet. Chester did a cartwheel and cut his second finger severely on his ice ax. They dug themselves out, stopped Chester's bleeding and bandaged his hand.

The avalanche was 300 feet wide and 18 inches deep and the runout was 1,000 feet below the fracture line. The climbers continued down to the landing strip where Chester received medical care from the High Latitude Research Program.

Given their situation, at the top of a storm-loaded pass and without food so that they could wait for the slopes to settle, there was nothing else they could have done.

In June 1981, in a similar accident, three climbers were

descending from 16,200 feet on the West Buttress because one member of the group was sick. Six feet of new powder snow had fallen in the previous two days. Just below the fixed lines, the slope in front of the lead climber avalanched, and all three were pulled down for 600 feet. They were half buried in the light snow, but were able to dig themselves out. Juan Hoyos' ax had cut his face and punctured his groin. At 14,300 feet, an Army doctor closed Hoyos' facial wound with 15 stitches; then he walked down to the landing strip.

Although it's obvious that travelling on freshly storm-loaded slopes of 20 to 35 degrees can be unsafe, climbers like Hoyos have no choice if they're sick, out of food or must move while the weather permits. Nevertheless, there are places that can be avoided during unstable weather conditions. More than once, groups have camped at 15,400 feet on the West Buttress (directly under the slope leading to the fixed line) and have had their tents buried when the slope above avalanched spontaneously. Tents should be pitched as far from the fixed-line basin as possible.

In June 1982, the Valley Mountaineers and the North Cascades Alpine School (NCAS) set up camp at 12,500 feet on the West Buttress route. Meanwhile, Fantasy Ridge and Mountain Trip guided groups cached some gear nearby. That night, wet snow fell at the rate of one inch per hour and the winds were out of the southeast at 25 miles per hour. This was an unusual situation. The 40- to 60-degree slopes were being loaded with wet snow that didn't slide off and continued to collect until morning. Very early in the morning, the two groups camped at 12,500 feet heard avalanches coming down the gullies from the West Buttress. At 6:30 A.M., an avalanche from a large bowl on the slopes above was funnelled down a gully towards their four tents. It buried them under two to four feet of wet snow. The members of the Valley Mountaineers group were thrown out of their tents and one of them was buried for 20 minutes. As they had lost their shovels in the avalanche, the NCAS group dug the climber out. Although two tents were destroyed, no one was injured. The NCAS group continued up the mountain, while the Valley Mountaineers retreated. The Mountain Trip group found their cache and continued their climb. However, despite extensive digging and probing, the Fantasy Ridge group couldn't find theirs and two of the members retreated. (In 1978, an avalanche hit the Courtney–Skinner group at this site.)

Although the word has gotten out about this site, parties continue to camp here and be hit by avalanches. On July 7, 1987, a Rainier Mountaineering group camped at 12,700 feet because one of the clients was altitude sick and could not continue to 14,300 feet. It snowed that night.

At 5:30 A.M., a 60-yard-wide slab avalanche ran for 300 yards and covered four of their five tents with several feet of debris. They immediately began digging one another out. The last person to be dug out was hypothermic, while one digger had a frostbitten finger; others coughed up blood from the exertion of digging or from bruised lungs incurred while buried in the debris. After probing and recovering everything except two ice axes and a harness, they descended to the landing strip.

Even though the bergschrund at 12,900 feet was buried that year, it could easily have been dug out for a fine campsite. It is extraordinary that guides—who are paid to avoid such situations—continually subject their clients to the hazards of the windswept, avalanche-prone basin, while just several hundred feet above, lies a safe bergschrund. It is only a matter of time before someone is killed in an avalanche here.

On May 26, 1990, just above and around the corner from the 12,500-foot bergschrund, a football-sized rock struck Dwight

Percy on his left hip. With help from his companions, he continued up to 14,300 feet and was flown out several days later. At Humana Hospital in Anchorage, he was treated for fractures of the left ilium and the pubic ramis bone. Although this is an unusual accident, other parties coming around Windy Corner should watch for similar rockfalls or wet snowslides—particularly on warm summer afternoons.

The most dangerous avalanche zone on the entire mountain is the Wickersham Wall. After the first ascent, Hans Gmoser remarked that his group could not have survived a large snowstorm on the upper part of the route. Along with many dangerous, low-angled snow deposition zones, the face is pockmarked with unpredictable hanging glaciers and seracs.

On June 4, 1988, while en route to the Wickersham Wall, four Italian climbers skied over Kahiltna Pass. They went down the north ridge, then off the ridge to look for a safe route down in the deep snow deposited by a recent storm. Suddenly a 200-foot-wide avalanche broke beneath three of the climbers, who were unroped and on skis. Two were swept out, while Marco Pedrolini was carried down toward Peters Basin and into a crevasse—most of the debris then swept over Pedrolini. He climbed out, unhurt.

The foursome lost most of their gear in the avalanche. Badly shaken, they climbed back over the pass and out to the landing strip. Certainly luck played a factor in their survival. The climbers had already been warned by the Rangers about that summer's excessive snowfalls and extreme avalanche conditions. Smart climbers—after observing heavy snowfalls and receiving warnings—would simply abandon their route and climb the safer West Buttress instead.

The Northeast Fork of the Kahiltna Glacier also rates high in objective dangers. Aside from crevasses, the valley is fringed

Avalanche coming over the Cassin Ridge. *GARY KOFINAS*

with hanging glaciers and seracs. As it is a relatively narrow valley, many climbers have watched avalanches roar across the breadth of the glacier. Only two tent sites on the approaches to the West Rib and the Cassin can be considered marginally safe. One is on the top of a small hill, just before the icefall which curves up around the West Rib. The second, above the icefall at 11,600 feet, hugs the eastern side of the valley in order to avoid the potential slide path of a hanging glacier on the Southwest Face.

In July 1980, the Toronto Cassin Expedition started up the Northeast Fork of the Kahiltna. Although they carried a CB radio, they were never heard from or seen again despite 300 man hours of aerial searching. As of winter 1982–83, their bodies had not been found: the area has become known as the "Valley of Death."

Mike Helms wrote about the avalanche that he experienced while camping at about 9,000 feet on the Northeast Fork in June 1980:

> June 5 started out as a lovely day. We were all four up early, enjoying the morning sunshine as an opportunity to dry our bags and to warm ourselves. I was savoring my second or third cup of coffee when I heard a loud crack from the icefall on the Kahiltna Peaks immediately behind us. I looked to my right and saw Bob running across the glacier. I glanced back to my left and it seemed the whole side of the Kahiltna Peaks were in motion. That's when I started running. Simon [McCartney] and Jack [Roberts] were still in their tent. They were totally obscured by a wall of snow. I do remember covering my face to make an air pocket and saying to myself, "Oh! Christ, not now, not like this." As the snow began to clear, I saw Bob walking back to camp. Both of us were white with snowdust. We were getting a good laugh out of our sprint

when we walked into camp. What we saw when the dust cleared sobered us up immediately.

The avalanche had stopped a short six feet from our tents. It was the largest ice avalanche I had ever seen. Maybe a mile in width by a half mile; some of the blocks were as large as pickup trucks. The spot where Bob had originally stopped was buried under six to eight feet of cement-hard rubble! Jack's sleeping bag was drying in one of the tents. The air blast from the avalanche blew it nearly a quarter of a mile out onto the glacier.

Because of trail-breaking difficulties and tedious route-finding through the crevasses or whiteouts, many climbers, like Helms, camp beneath hanging glaciers, not realizing that they are in a danger zone. In 1981, because of a whiteout, I camped at the same site as Helms. The next morning when it cleared, I was horrified to see that we were in the runout path of a hanging glacier. If we had camped another mile up the glacier, we would have been safe.

Some parties follow the original Cassin approach up the longer East Fork of the Kahiltna to avoid the more dangerous Valley of Death approach. Although the East Fork is wider and safer, it is still hazardous. In July 1982, a Norwegian party observed a tremendous serac avalanche sweep down from Peak 12,240, across the glacier, to within yards of their camp on the west side of the East Fork of the Kahiltna.

The preeminent, nightmarish hanging glacier on Denali is to be found at the upper end of the East Fork. It is perched at 16,000 feet on the South Face, and is three quarters of a mile wide and 300 feet high. It has been dubbed "Big Bertha," like its relative on the Khumbu Icefall on Mount Everest which was named after the Nazi artillery cannon.

Big Bertha releasing in a continuous 4000-foot wave down the South
Face. *Michael Covington*

Climber on a South Buttress cornice. *GARY KOFINAS*

During Mark Hesse's solo ascent of the South Face, Big Bertha released five minutes after he had reached the bergschrund, just beyond the path of the airborne avalanche.

Climbers on the nearby South Buttress should proceed with caution on the ramp between 12,000 and 15,500 feet where a hanging glacier and seracs threaten the entire route. The ramp is also quite dangerous after snowstorms. Tent sites should be chosen with care.

In July 1967, the South Buttress team supporting the American Direct South Face party had just descended the ramp from 12,000 feet onto the East Fork. A serac at 15,000 feet on the ramp collapsed, and the debris from the avalanche buried two members of the team up to their waists. The other two were blown 40 yards into a crevasse.

In July 1981, a probable avalanche buried a Japanese team in the East Fork. Makoto Kinoshita, Masuaki Ohnishi and Osamu Ozaki had planned to climb the American Direct route. As they had already climbed the West Buttress in June, they were well acclimatized and knew what to expect.

They were last seen at 9,200 feet on the East Fork by Mike Covington, who was dragging out a frostbitten client. At that time, "the walls were coming down all over the glacier." Sometimes they had to stop talking because the roaring was so loud. Covington told the Japanese that his group "barely got away with their lives" and that "it was suicide to go up there" after such a big snowstorm. They said they would "go have a look" anyway. Another storm system moved in. Two weeks later, after it cleared, the National Park Service began search flights for the Japanese team.

Covington felt that they never made it to the start of the climb and that they were hit by an avalanche on the glacier. The only trace of the group was a tent they had left pitched on the

Kahiltna Glacier. It is likely that the Japanese continued because of peer pressure. As Covington had warned them, they knew the route was dangerous, but probably wanted to prove they could do it despite the odds against them.

In all potential avalanche situations, a conservative attitude, common sense and prior avalanche training are invaluable. Heavy snowfall, with or without wind, turns many slopes into deathtraps for at least 24 hours after a storm has abated. Wide variations in temperature, in the morning or evening, can also cause unstable conditions. If possible, routes underneath hanging glaciers should be avoided or sprinted through. Although few climbers on Denali carry avalanche beacons, they could help to save lives. Ski-pole probes and large snow shovels are also essential for digging out avalanche victims.

However, regardless of the precautions taken, luck still determines the outcome on some routes. The fact that seven climbers have been completely buried, without a trace, illustrates how large avalanches can be and how minuscule climbers are in comparison. Denali avalanches are deadly.

SUMMARY: AVALANCHES

DATE	NAME	ROUTE & ELEVATION OF INCIDENT	COMMENTS
5/19/78	CARMICHAEL AAPORTA	W RIB 12500	WITHIN 24 HOURS AFTER SNOWFALL
1978	COURTNEY SKINNER	W BUTTRESS 12500	DANGEROUS CAMP
6/5/80	HELMS	NE FORK 9000	DANGEROUS CAMP
7/80	CARROLL CHASE MANSON LEWIS	NE FORK OR CASSIN *	DANGEROUS GLACIER
5/81	COVINGTON	W RIB 12000	WITHIN 24 HOURS AFTER SNOWFALL
7/19/81	HOYOS	W BUTTRESS 15000	WITHIN 24 HOURS AFTER SNOWFALL
7/81	KINOSHITA OHNISHI OZAKI	E FORK OR AMERICAN DIRECT *	WITHIN 24 HOURS AFTER LARGE SNOWFALL
5/18/82	*	W RIB 12000	SWEPT OFF BY PARTY ABOVE
6/6/82	CHESTER READ FLETCHER	S BUTTRESS 12000	WITHIN 24 HOURS AFTER SNOWFALL
6/16/82	VALLEY MTNRS., N CASCADES ALPINE	W BUTTRESS 12500	DANGEROUS CAMP

AVALANCHES

HOW EVACUATED	RESULT	RESCUED BY	GOVERNMENT COST
AIRPLANE, HELICOPTER	2 BROKEN ANKLES	NPS	$4450
*	*		NONE
	UNHURT		NONE
BODIES NEVER RECOVERED	4 DEATHS	AIR FORCE, TALKEETNA AIR, AKLAND, ERA	$13987.62
	UNHURT		NONE
ON FOOT	ICE AX WOUND, 15 STITCHES		NONE
BODIES NEVER RECOVERED	3 DEATHS	*	$2575.65
	UNHURT		NONE
ON FOOT	WOUND FROM ICE AX		NONE
	UNHURT		NONE

*INDICATES INFORMATION NOT AVAILABLE

181

C H A P T E R

U n u s u a l   A c c i d e n t s

*Great adventures are possible
on Mount McKinley. . . . providing
those who attempt the mountains
have served their long climbing
apprenticeships first.*

Doug Scott in
ALASKA MAGAZINE, MAY 1977

Psychological problems, abscessed teeth, diabetes, knee problems and general physical unpreparedness are but a few of the problems that can flare up out of all proportion on Denali. Because of the subzero air, high altitude and stressful living conditions, any small medical problem can develop into a liability. Even well-prepared guides have been blown off the West Buttress in their tents—twice! Although seldom diagnosed, gastroenteritis and carbon monoxide poisoning have plagued climbers on Denali for decades. However, in recent years, climbers have died or been evacuated because of them.

Prior Health Problems On May 22, 1981, Steve Gall and I were guiding a seven-member party for Fantasy Ridge Expeditions on the West Buttress route. One of the clients, Ernest Chandler (49), could not travel without taking a rest every five or ten minutes because he was unfit and overweight. Although Gall took his drag sled and most of the weight from his pack,

Chandler continued to take frequent rest stops. Towards the end of the day, after going up a hill at 7,600 feet, Chandler collapsed with a pain in his chest and was barely able to breathe.

As his wife, Evelyn, had panicked, I separated her from her husband. Then I calmed Chandler down, asked him to breathe slowly and relax, and put him in his sleeping bag. His pulse was high (92 per minute). There was pain in his chest when he took a deep breath and he had a headache. It also appeared that he might have a more serious problem, such as a pulmonary embolism or a heart condition. He confided to me that he had high blood pressure and had neglected to take his medicine that day.

That night, I slept next to Chandler and monitored his vital signs. I gave him warm drinks and a Valium capsule to help him relax. His pulse dropped to a normal 68. In the morning, he insisted that he should continue up the mountain. I decreed that he should neither continue nor walk back down to the landing strip, as I felt that he might collapse again. I was unwilling to take the responsibility for a client on the glacier who was overweight and had high blood pressure. Gall and I arranged to have him flown out, and Doug Geeting was able to taxi his plane right up to our tent, on a flat stretch of glacier at 7,600 feet.

Although I had asked for medical information on all of the clients prior to the trip, it was not available. Many guide companies have no real way of screening their clients until they arrive on the mountain. After Chandler flew off the mountain, he saw a doctor who diagnosed exhaustion; later that year, he was operated on for a ventral hernia. He came back the following summer and caused a considerable problem because he couldn't carry his share of the weight. He made it to 14,300 feet, but was a liability again.

In June 1982, a client in Michael Covington's Fantasy Ridge expedition, who had an unstable mental history, began talking about jumping off Kahiltna Pass and killing herself. Steve Gall accompanied her down to base camp where she became psychotic. At one point, she had to be restrained and was eventually sedated with Valium. Doug Geeting made a risky pickup in poor weather and flew her to the hospital. Her history of psychosis should have disqualified her from the trip.

Clients should present a full, accurate picture of the state of their health and be carefully screened by their guides. Hopefully, guides on Denali will not have to deal with such prior health problems in the future.

On April 24, 1976, Jon Kushner, a diabetic, froze his two types of insulin at 14,300 feet on the West Buttress. After a radio miscommunication about the severity of his condition, he was evacuated by airplane from 10,000 feet on April 28 as he was descending to base camp. Although, apparently, Kushner could have made it down by himself, another party radioed (as often happens) that he needed an airlift.

He should, however, have taken better precautions against having his insulin freeze. The potential for insulin's freezing should be sufficiently obvious that any diabetic would insulate it inside a shirt or a sleeping bag.

In early July 1976, Gerhard Biederman was separated from his insulin at 10,000 feet by a three-day storm. When the group returned to camp after the storm, Biederman was in good shape, but was given too much insulin and went into insulin shock. Jim Sharp made an emergency landing and evacuated him to Providence Hospital in Anchorage.

As climbers are frequently pinned down by storms on Denali,

Biederman should have taken this into account and carried his insulin with him.

In July 1974, the leader of a four-man party was unable to descend below 15,000 feet on the Harper Glacier. He was evacuated by helicopter. At the hospital, he was diagnosed with a septic-arthritic knee. Heavy packs can turn climbers with prior knee problems into basket cases.

Dental health is another concern. In July 1973, a client of Ray Genet's was evacuated from 14,300 feet with an abscessed tooth. Dozens of other climbers have also come to grief on Denali because of dental problems. As minor toothaches can develop into major jaw pain at high altitude, dental checkups are essential prior to climbing Denali. Certainly this client's evacuation could have been prevented if he had simply gone to the dentist before the expedition.

Does it make sense to attempt Denali while affected by a small medical problem? Why reduce one's likelihood of success, jeopardize other climbers, and cause pilots to risk their lives for you—all because of your inability to consult a physician before leaving? Even then, a clean bill of health is no assurance you'll get up Denali unscathed.

Exhaustion On May 15, 1980, two Germans, Manfred Loibl and Margaret Huschke, arrived in Talkeetna. The couple were on holiday in Alaska and had not initally planned to climb Denali. This lack of planning may have contributed to their poor state of preparedness and their eventual deaths. Few people, if any, have climbed Denali on impulse, and these two underestimated the seriousness of the undertaking. They rented vapor barrier boots and crampons and borrowed snowshoes. Pilots Doug Geeting and Sonny Kragness were both concerned about their insufficient equipment. When Kragness asked if they had contacted the National Park Service Rangers, they replied that "their papers were in order." Because the two were from out of town and were probably not familiar with the regulations, they had not registered with the rangers. It is also unlikely that they had very much information about the mountain. They were flown in that day.

Reports from the mountain indicated that Loibl was very strong and that Huschke could barely keep up with him. On May 25, they made it to 17,200 feet. They went to the summit two days later.

Another German climber, who met them at 19,500 feet, reported that they were exhausted and had asked him for food. Later, a guided party of Germans who met them just below the summit at 4:30 P.M. noted that the two were extremely exhausted. The weather was deteriorating and, at 5 P.M., when the group started down, they asked Loibl and Huschke if they would like to rope up with them. The two declined, however, saying that they preferred to rest a little longer.

Loibl and Huschke did not return to 17,200 feet that night; the weather become very bad, with high winds. Another climber, Mike McComb, who spent a miserable bivouac at 19,000 feet on the West Buttress the same night, did not see the couple. Two days later, when the weather cleared, Ranger Dave Buchanan spotted Loibl and Huschke's lifeless forms at 19,300 feet from an airplane.

On July 2, when guide Brian Okonek placed their bodies in a crevasse, he noticed that Loibl had a bruise on his forehead. It is likely that the exhausted couple sat down in the storm and died of hypothermia. Although they did carry a shovel to dig in with, they carried no food for their summit attempt, which probably contributed to their exhaustion. It would be fair to say that Loibl and Huschke grossly underestimated the mountain

This climber collapsed and died at 19,300 feet; the body is one of more than 25 that remain on the mountain. *MIKE GRABER*

and overestimated their own abilities. A Denali climb takes a tremendous amount of physical and mental preparation: an impulsive ascent is foolhardy.

In 1976, two climbers nearly met a similar fate. In their preclimb correspondence with the National Park Service, the leader wrote, "One of our members wants to be dumped in a crevasse (if he dies, that is) and for us to go on. What's the legality of this?" This was an unusual and, in light of what was to happen, prophetic letter. Such a casual attitude toward dying could well be the cause of many accidents on Denali.

On May 10, at 4:30 A.M., four members of the expedition started for the summit from 17,200 feet on the West Buttress. They reached Denali Pass at 10:30 A.M. and continued up to 19,500 feet, arriving there at around 5 P.M. Their water bottles had frozen at Denali Pass. Two of the climbers were tired and decided to descend. The other two continued to the summit and bivouacked within 200 feet of the top. As they had lost both bivouac sacks, they spent a very cold night and could not operate their stove.

By morning, one of them had severely frozen hands. They descended, taking a bad fall, and spent a second night out at 19,500 feet. They were discovered by Dougal Haston and Doug Scott, who were descending the West Buttress after a grueling climb of the South Face and an uncomfortable bivouaac on the summit. They were too exhausted to help the pair, but descended to 17,200 feet and notified the rest of their party. (It is interesting to note that an overwhelming majority of the climbers who bivouac near the summit bring themselves to the point of exhaustion. This can lead to hypothermia, frostbite and, sometimes, death. The combination of cold and altitude should preclude bivouacs above 18,000 feet.)

Fortunately, two other members of the party were able to

assist the pair down that day. All four of the climbers involved in the summit attempt were flown out from 14,300 feet the next day. The two who spent two nights out above 19,000 feet lost extensive portions of their hands and feet. One had worn tight-fitting neoprene socks which probably contributed to the severity of his frostbite.

It had taken them six hours to go from 17,200 feet to Denali Pass, a trip that normally takes three hours at most. At that point, they should have turned back. Their frozen water bottles could have been insulated under their shirts; this would have helped to prevent dehydration and, in turn, exhaustion and frostbite. Their subsequent altitude sickness affected their judgment. It was only luck that prevented them from being buried in a crevasse (as they had inquired about in their preclimb letter).

On May 18, 1988, a Genet Expeditions client, Lynne Salerno (31), couldn't keep up with her companions as they walked to the summit. Earlier, assistant guide John Schweider, had turned back with two other weaker clients—taking the sleeping bag with him. The head guide, Vern Tejas, allowed the remaining clients, Moss and Kazel, to go up, while he waited with Salerno. After a short rest, Salerno convinced Tejas that she was okay, so they continued up. On the summit ridge, Tejas noticed that her cheek was white with frostbite.

As Schweider descended below Denali Pass, he fell (possibly pulled by his clients) and was unable to self-arrest. He went 75 feet and cracked his head on some rocks. The clients assisted him down to 17,200 feet.

Meanwhile, just below the summit, Salerno was exhausted and had difficulty keeping her balance. Eventually, she became incoherent and was unable to walk. Meanwhile, the winds picked up and the temperature dropped. Tejas dug a trench. Leaving Salerno there with the two inexperienced and exhausted

193

clients, he descended to get a bivy bag and stove that were cached below.

Shortly after being placed in the trench, Salerno stopped breathing. When Tejas returned, he confirmed that she was dead, then took Moss and Kazel back to 17,200 feet. Salerno's body was abandoned to the mountain. Moss (who eventually lost a piece of his thumb and big toe to frostbite) and Schweider (who sustained a compression fracture of the lumbar vertebrae and lacerations) were both helicoptered out the next day.

Tejas is one of the more experienced guides on Denali. In retrospect, his allowing Salerno to achieve her goals was commendable, yet dangerous. Salerno had no symptoms of altitude sickness, and just seemed to be moving too slowly. However, she never told Tejas her previous medical history. Because of brain damage suffered in a childhood illness, Salerno was impervious to pain and cold. Furthermore, other difficulties had made her a rare overachiever—one who never turned back for anything. Although Salerno had the option of descending with Schweider, she didn't take it.

Nonetheless, Tejas' actions represent the requisite pattern of most serious accidents on Denali: the group split up; bivouac gear was taken down or left where it was of little use; they continued up very late in the day, while all other parties on the mountain were descending; reaching the summit became a bigger priority than it should have.

Clearly, Salerno was an unusual person, a client difficult for any guide to read. In the end, she was the one who ran out of gas—even her parents recognized that, due to their daughter's medical history and "never-quit" personality, Tejas was not at fault. It is amazing that such accidents don't happen more often on Denali, particularly to guides.

Gastroenteritis, Carbon Monoxide Poisoning A year later, another accident prophetically demonstrated the importance of environmental concerns on Denali. After descending the West Buttress route, Tetumi Inoue was sledded out on May 24, 1989, from 9,800 feet with severe abdominal pains; he had been unable to eat since the previous evening. He became semiconscious and his abdomen was rigid. He was flown out that evening and underwent surgery the next day.

Similar gastroenteritis has struck other climbers on Denali over the last decade. Quite probably, Inoue's problem emanated from ingesting fecal matter after melting snow water at 14,300 or 17,200 feet. Fecal contamination of snow is a serious problem on the West Buttress and other popular routes—although most parties use plastic bags and dispose of their waste in crevasses, people are still getting sick.

The first accurately diagnosed case of carbon monoxide poisoning occurred in 1985. Raymond Weinrich and Charles Wolf were both fatigued when they reached 17,200 feet on the West Buttress. While Weinrich moved into an igloo occupied by a climber who spent most of the evening cooking, Wolf set up his tent outside; Weinrich could not sleep because of his headache.

In the morning, Wolf found Weinrich incapacitated and crying due to his severe headache. Ranger Scott Gill examined Weinrich and recorded his pulse at 120 per minute, with respirations of 26 per minute. Gill immediately moved the victim out of the poorly ventilated igloo and into the tent, then administered bottled oxygen and fluids. Although the weather was deteriorating, Wolf's condition improved in a matter of hours. Gill walked Wolf down to 14,300 feet, buffeted by 30- to 40-mph winds. At the medical camp, Dr. Peter Hackett diagnosed carbon monoxide poisoning.

195

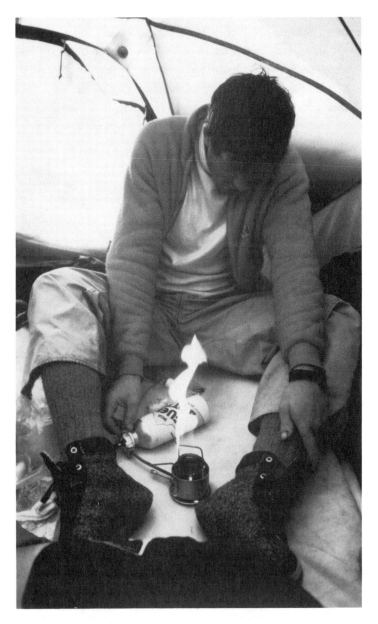

Improper tent ventilation while starting a stove. JONATHAN WATERMAN

Gill's immediate response and descent was exemplary. It is tricky for nonphysicians to diagnose carbon monoxide poisoning because HACE exhibits similar symptoms. Furthermore, carbon monoxide poisoning could possibly predispose climbers to both HACE and HAPE. In Weinrich's case, his immediate recovery seemed to rule out HACE. More importantly, carbon monoxide poisoning can be prevented by cooking in well-ventilated areas. In an igloo or snow cave there should be a fist-sized breathing hole directly above the stove; cooking inside tents should not be considered unless the door is zipped wide open.

Sometimes it is difficult to cook with an open door—as proven by two Swiss climbers the following summer. Although Rolf Rauber and Bruno Beyeler had been warned by their companions to ventilate their two-man tent, on the evening of June 7, the pair cooked with the tent flaps closed as ten-mph gusts blew snow around their tent, which was surrounded by four-foot snow walls.

The next morning, Rauber and Beyeler were both found cold, unconscious and pulseless. Their butane stove had been left on. Although a pot of soup had boiled over, they may also have been using the stove to keep the tent warm—an inadvisable technique. The stove had run for nearly three hours. Sometime during the night, both men had simply fallen asleep from the effects of carbon monoxide poisoning, then died. If the 22 and 23 year olds had heeded the repeated warnings of their companions and Park Rangers about ventilating their tent while cooking, they would still be alive today. Normally, cooking in tents is considered unsafe, particularly given the potential for fires. But sometimes long-lasting storms on Denali allow climbers few options.

West Buttress Tent Blowdowns The stock joke on Denali concerns those unfortunate parties whose tents sail away like kites.

Two climbers at 16,800 feet on the West Buttress.
JONATHAN WATERMAN

On a blustery summer day in 1983, a dome tent, replete with down sleeping bags, blew past climbers camped at 8,000 feet. An hour later, the sheepish owners of the tent (they had neglected to stake it down at their 10,000-foot camp), skied by and asked which way it had gone. These incidents seem to recur amongst guided parties.

In 1989, however, tents were blown off the mountain with more serious consequences. On May 27, assistant guide John Richards and clients Jim Johnson and Howard Tuthill were blown, tent and all, from their 16,400-foot campsite off the northside of the ridge. Richards came out of the tent 200 feet below camp, while Johnson and Tuthill fell 1,000 feet. Richards was unhurt; he climbed back up to camp and alerted head guide Dave Staeheli, who immediately radioed for help and secured the other tents. He then set off to rescue his clients, carrying a sleeping bag, warm fluids, a stove and a first aid kit, and bracing himself in 50- to 60-mph winds.

Staeheli found the two clinging to an ice ledge, hypothermic, with assorted injuries, and dressed only in their underwear. Making them as warm as possible, he reascended the ridge and called for more help and equipment. Eventually, the climbers were somewhat stabilized. Sixteen hours after their fall, a helicopter balanced on the small ledge, picked up Johnson and Tuthill, and flew them to Anchorage. Johnson was treated for contusions of the kidney, while Tuthill had fractured a vertebra; both men had frostbitten fingers and toes.

Although their tent had a dozen anchors, their three-foot snow walls extended only partway around it. Although many climbers have safely made do with less wall protection, higher walls might have prevented the tent from blowing away. The ridge crest from 16,000 to 16,800 feet is more exposed to winds than anywhere else on the West Buttress. Most climbers remain fully dressed during such storms, even in the tent; this would have lessened their problems after the fall. And future climbers would be wise to avoid placing their tents on the ridge crest altogether and to dig snow caves instead. At the very least, they should build higher and more complete snow walls.

Later that summer, guides Craig John and Curt Hewitt pitched their tents at 16,100 feet, just above the top of the fixed line. After two days of storms, John said that their "tent [was] like a spaceship about to take off." He then went to help his clients shovel out their tents.

Meanwhile, as Hewitt was putting on his boots, the tent floor billowed up. He threw himself on the floor in an attempt to hold it down, but the tent blew over the three- to four-foot walls and carried him 100 yards down the slope. While he was halfway out the snow portal, another gust carried him 50 yards. He stopped, nearly got free, then was blown another 50 yards. When he finally got free, he tried to hold the tent down, but had to let go because he was getting hypothermic.

Wearing one boot and no gloves, Hewitt climbed back to camp; he was hypothermic, but uninjured. Two days later, when the winds let up, the team descended.

In this case, snow walls were adequate, but only two ice axes and one picket were used to shore the tent down. One ice ax popped out, while the other ice ax and the picket stayed—but the tent loops ripped off. Without building complete snow walls and placing multiple anchors, even the best made tents can become kites.

SUMMARY: UNUSUAL ACCIDENTS

DATE	NAME	ROUTE & ELEVATION OF INCIDENT	COMMENTS
7/31/73	BAKER	W BUTTRESS 14300	ABSCESSED TOOTH, NO PRIOR DENTAL CHECKUP
7/31/74	LEWITT	HARPER 15000	SEPTIC-ARTHRITIC KNEE, PRIOR HISTORY
4/28/76	KUSHNER	W BUTTRESS 14300	DIABETIC SHOCK, INSULIN FROZE
5/10/76	THOMPSON WILLIS	W BUTTRESS 20000	DEHYDRATION, EXHAUSTION, 2 HIGH BIVOUACS
7/5/76	BIEDERMAN	W BUTTRESS 10000	INSULIN SHOCK, SEPARATED FROM INSULIN, OVERDOSE
5/27/80	LOIBL HUSCHKE	W BUTTRESS 19500	ILL-PREPARED, EXHAUSTION, HYPOTHERMIA
5/22/81	CHANDLER	W BUTTRESS 7600	OVERWEIGHT, HIGH BLOOD PRESSURE, COLLAPSE
6/13/82	FANTASY RIDGE CLIENT	W BUTTRESS 10000	PSYCHOSIS
5/24/89	TETUML INOUE	W BUTTRESS 9800	GASTROENTERITIS
5/29/85	RAYMOND WEINRICH	W BUTTRESS 17200	CARBON MONOXIDE POISONING, POORLY VENTED CAVE
6/7/86	ROLF RAUBER AND BRUNO BEYELER	W BUTTRESS 14300	CARBON MONOXIDE POISONING, UNVENTED TENT
5/27/89	JIM JOHNSON AND HOWARD TUTHILL	W BUTTRESS 16400	TENT BLOWN OFF

HOW EVACUATED	RESULT	RESCUED BY	GOVERNMENT COST
HELICOPTER	RECOVERED	ARMY	$1000
HELICOPTER	*	NPS	$2000
HELICOPTER	*	ARMY	$3912
HELICOPTER	FROSTBITE EXTENSIVE AMPUTATION	ARMY	$3249
AIRPLANE	*	JIM SHARP	NONE
BURIED ON MOUNTAIN	2 DEATHS	TALKEETNA AIR TAXI	$303
AIRPLANE	VENTRAL HERNIA OPERATION	TALKEETNA AIR TAXI	NONE
ON FOOT	*	TALKEETNA AIR TAXI	NONE
SLEDDED OUT	RECOVERY	SELF	NONE
ON FOOT	RECOVERY	NPS	NONE
	DEATHS	OWN PARTY, NPS	$3981
HELICOPTER	FROSTBITE, FRACTURED VERTEBRAE, BRUISED KIDNEY	SOLOY HELICOPTERS	$8678

*INDICATES INFORMATION NOT AVAILABLE

How to Prepare for Denali

*Not a single mishap had occurred
to mar the complete success
of our undertaking—not an injury
of anyone, nor an illness.*

Hudson Stuck in
THE ASCENT OF DENALI

Even though this chapter does not discuss a specific category of accident, as do the preceding chapters, careful preparation for an expedition to Denali can in itself be a major factor in preventing many types of accidents.

In 1967, Boyd N. Everett, Jr. wrote *Organization of an Alaskan Expedition*. Although it was never formally published during his lifetime, this widely read report has been highly regarded over the years as the best source of information on preparing an expedition to the Alaskan peaks. This chapter is based upon that report, and some of the information is taken directly from Everett's material.

Sources, services and references pertaining to the topics in this chapter are listed in the appendices. Appendix referrals are noted in the text.

TEAM

Choosing a Team Boyd N. Everett, Jr. wrote that probably the most important factor in choosing a party for an expedition is that each man be congenial and able to live with every other man under strenuous conditions for a period of weeks. Social compatibility is essential. Almost never will it pay to take the exceptionally strong, but humorless and unresponsive, technician over a congenial but less technically-oriented man. For most routes, it is probably best to have a party of similar technical ability and physical strength. Having climbers of about the same age may be desirable, particularly if the group is young. On potentially difficult routes, it might be desirable to have a few men of exceptional ability for the difficult leading.

Experience   Each climber should be seasoned in winter mountaineering, have experience in first aid and a thorough understanding of crevasse rescue. Everyone should be familiar with altitude-related problems, and more than one person in the group should have some avalanche schooling. Prior cardiovascular training, such as running, biking, ski-racing, swimming or hiking with a heavy pack, can improve one's performance on the mountain. Good campcraft (snow caving, cooking and backpacking skills) is an essential part of a Denali trip, perhaps even more so than technical climbing ability.

Party Size   The optimal team size is four members, although experienced, expeditionary mountaineers often climb in two-man teams. A party of three or four has greater strength in terms of lead climbing, trail breaking and self-rescue capabilities. The larger the party, the more safely and slowly it will move.

Leadership   Every party has its own conception of leadership. Two-man teams have the fewest problems with respect to leadership decisions, while large expeditions can spend an entire day negotiating. Although some parties act democratically, many groups (usually foreign) elect one member who is more experienced and respected than the rest to be the leader. The leader's responsibility must be agreed upon before the team gets to the mountain. The best leaders are good followers and only make themselves heard when the situation demands it. Guided expeditions, however, have been observed to work well under somewhat authoritative guide-leaders, who would be considered abrasive under any other circumstances.

Guides Many individuals choose to hire a guide because of their lack of familiarity with the mountain, time constraints that prevent them from planning the trip properly, or their inexperience.

Denali National Park and Preserve has issued six concessionaire guide permits and one educational use permit. These guide services are listed in Appendix F.

Solo Climbs Although many routes on Denali have been soloed, most of the climbers involved made arrangements to travel roped to others on crevassed glacier approaches. For the vast majority of Denali aspirants, soloing would be suicidal for obvious reasons. One of the most experienced climbers in the Alaska Range was killed in a solo attenpt in 1981.

ROUTE PLANNING

Information and Resources There is a great deal of information available on Denali routes. To begin with, *High Alaska*, published by The American Alpine Club, will be a useful resource. *The American Alpine Journal* publishes route descriptions and photographs almost every year. Excellent black and white photographs are available from the Museum of Science in Boston. *The Canadian Alpine Journal, Climbing, Rock and Ice, Mountain* and *The Mountain World* all contain fine photographs of and articles about Denali. (See Appendix G.)

Route Recommendations Denali is attempted by over a thousand climbers per year. More than half of them choose the West Buttress, while the West Rib, the Muldrow and the Cassin Ridge are next in order of popularity. Beginning expeditionary mountaineers should consider the Muldrow or West Buttress routes. The 1954 South Buttress or the Pioneer Ridge would be fine choices for mountaineers with expeditionary and cold weather experience who are looking for isolated, nontechnical routes. Experienced, expeditionary climbers have a wide range of routes to choose from. The South and East Buttresses harbor many difficult variations with no traffic to contend with. If fixed ropes are being considered, an easier route should be chosen instead.

Route Times Whereas climbers often overestimate the pure technical difficulty of a route, there is a definite tendency to underestimate how many days it will take to climb a given route. Climbers accustomed to looking at 2,000- and 3,000-foot walls in the Canadian Rockies will have difficulty gauging distances when they look at photographs of Alaska's 8,000- to 10,000-foot (and higher) vertical rises. Even when the mountains are properly evaluated for size, climbers overestimate their ability to move on them. There are several reasons for this. For many climbers, there are initial psychological barriers that prevent them from working efficiently. Uncertainty about climbing and avalanche conditions is also a factor. Low-altitude climbing done at night will require more time than if done during the day. On the bigger mountains, altitude will slow the party somewhat, particularly while backpacking. There is a tendency to underestimate the time required for camp chores. Meals usually require two hours or more to prepare. Breaking camp, including a meal, takes three to four hours. It shouldn't take this long, but it does. Six hours for eating and camp chores per day, plus eight hours for sleeping, leaves only ten hours per day, sometimes less, for actual climbing. This compares with 12 to 14 hours for most other mountains. Weather factors will often shorten many climbing days as well as decreasing the efficiency of the climbers.

Climbers leaving from the Southeast Fork of the Kahiltna should leave behind six days of food in case they're stormed in while waiting for a flight out. Even with bad weather, the climb should not take more than three and one half weeks from the landing strip. Under ideal conditions, parties have climbed the mountain in two weeks, although this is fast. Trying to climb Denali in less than two weeks might not allow for adequate acclimatization. Many beginning parties take more than four weeks because of superfluous supplies, excessive load ferrying and ponderous climbing styles.

DENALI NATIONAL PARK
AND PRESERVE

Requirements   In recent years, the National Park Service has loosened the old climbing requirements (radios, permission to climb, party size and experience levels) because they were ineffective and impossible to enforce. Now, the Park Service works mainly in advising climbers as well as coodinating rescues and cleaning up trash on the mountain. With the exception of some Fairbanks climbers, the majority of climbers have found that the requirements are quite simple and that they do not interfere with their climbing experience.

There are two requirements for expeditions planning climbs in Denali National Park and Preserve: 1. Expeditions to Denali and Mount Foraker must submit individual registrations to the mountaineering rangers prior to departure. (To avoid confusion, it is imperative that one team member handle all correspondence with the National Park Service, air carriers and support organizations. The name of the expedition should be used on all correspondence.) 2. Climbers should check in with the National Park Service Mountaineering Rangers in Talkeetna or at Denali Park Headquarters before and after the climb.

Rangers The Talkeetna Ranger Station is manned by the rangers from early April until late August. The Ranger Station is also a climbers' resource library with books, photographs, magazine articles and maps of the Alaska Range. The rangers are hired for their expertise on Denali, their rapport with climbers and their emergency medical and rescue backgrounds. They keep their fingers on the pulse of all Alaska Range activities by meeting all of the climbers, monitoring a CB radio in Talkeetna and performing regular climbing and cleanup patrols on the mountain.

RESCUE

Brian Okonek, a Denali climber and guide, wrote: "Far too many parties are crying wolf. This is a scary reality. A few false rescues and climbers, pilots and the National Park Service will begin to think that all rescue calls are hoaxes. This is going to cause the death of someone yet."

A team's self-sufficiency and ability to evacuate itself can mean life or death. Because of acclimatization problems, help from other parties is often nonexistent, and helicopters, for many reasons, are not always available.

The National Park Service (NPS) has refused helicopter evacuations to climbers who can safely be taken down the mountain. If the victim is dying and the weather is good, it can still take many hours, or even days, for the NPS to find a suitable helicopter with a willing pilot. Helicopters are often not insured for high-altitude landings. In the past, the NPS or the Army has paid the cost ($300–$13,000) of almost all rescues.

Rescue Procedure   Safety should be foremost in every climber's mind while preparing to attempt Denali. The author believes that most rescues are the result of secondary, obsessive factors (such as reaching the summit) that overshadow the primary consideration of coming back unscathed.

The following procedure is recommended for rescue: treat the victim until his condition is stable; if possible move the victim to a lower elevation immediately; radio the NPS for a helicopter if the victim's condition is deteriorating rapidly, or radio the base camp caretaker or a bush pilot to arrange for air evacuation from the lowest point to which the victim can safely be moved.

Approaches

Glacier Flying   From the south, the usual approach is by ski plane from Talkeetna to the Southeast Fork of the Kahiltna Glacier or to the Ruth Glacier. However, some groups walk or ski in from the George Parks Highway, a distance of about 100 miles.

Buses, limousines, planes and a train operate between Anchorage and Talkeetna. In Talkeetna, there are air services that fly climbers to either side of the mountain. As of 1991, round-trip flights average $225 per person. To guarantee a prompt flight in, it is best to make a reservation in advance and place a deposit. Climbers can sometimes wait up to ten days for the weather to clear so that the pilots can fly. From early May until late July, there is a radio caretaker, employed by the pilots, on the Southeast Fork of the Kahiltna Glacier who coordinates Talkeetna-bound flights and monitors Channel 19 on the CB radio 24 hours a day.

In addition to the Talkeetna pilots, there is one air service that will fly climbers to Kantishna, for approaches up the Peters or Muldrow glaciers. (See Appendix H.)

Dog Sled Reference   From the north, the Peters or Muldrow Glacier can be approached on skis or by dog sled. (See Appendix H.)

WEATHER

There is a popular belief that the weather in Alaska changes very rapidly. Although there are elements of truth in this statement, it needs clarification. From a relatively clear sky, a violent storm can appear within two hours. In such cases, however, telltale signs are almost always visible several hours ahead. Such signs would include long cloud streaks in the sky and lenticular caps over the high summits. (The summit must be avoided when these lenticular caps are on it.) When the weather is really clear, it rarely turns bad in less than 12 hours. A completely good weather day has a noticeable brightness in the air which a day of changing weather usually doesn't have. Good and bad weather tends to come in cycles. Good weather can last three to six days while bad conditions of ten consecutive days are not unusual. During this bad weather period, there will be some temporary clearings. Heavy clouds at lower or higher elevations on other mountains will indicate that the weather may return. When it does return, the change in condition can be sudden. At low elevation, usually not above 8,000 feet, climbers may also be annoyed by clouds that hang not more than 1,000 feet above the glacier. These clouds, which creep in off the ocean, bring whiteout and light rain or snow. They often appear when the weather higher on the mountain is excellent. These clouds, which are most common in July, can interfere with glacier flying and landings. It should be no surprise that wind will interfere with climbing more often than falling snow. If routes are marked with wands or if whiteout conditions aren't too bad, climbing can sometimes be done at low elevations even during snowstorms. When the wind does blow, however, it can be very violent, possibly up to 100 miles per hour at higher elevations. The prevailing wind will be from the south or southwest, but currents around the mountain can create strong gusts from any direction.

Snowfall will be heavy during storms. One to two feet of snow in a 24-hour period or three feet in two days is not unusual. It is normal to have a short break for a few hours after three days of continuous snow, but the storm can easily return after that break. Ten feet of powder snow in ten days is possible, although this would consolidate into perhaps five feet of solid snow. In general, there is no such thing as a partly cloudy day. Either the sky is clear or it snows.

It is probable that every mountain could be climbed in any month of the year, but some months are decidedly inhospitable for obvious reasons. Denali is one of the coldest mountains in the world because of its proximity to the Arctic Circle. From late April through August, it is not uncommon to experience temperatures of −30 degrees with 100 mph winds, whiteouts and ground blizzards. Conversely, the temperature can reach 80 degrees with slush puddles on the glacier. Several factors are important in deciding on dates for an Alaskan expedition. These are: hours of daylight, prevailing weather trends, and temperature ranges.

Hours of Daylight Between June 1 and July 15, there are nearly 24 hours of daylight in Alaska. The sun actually goes down for four hours, but the twilight is usually bright enough for all-night climbing. This has two important advantages. It permits evening climbing when daytime climbing would be hazardous because of sun-induced avalanche conditions. It also permits the climber to begin and end his day whenever he wants, and weather conditions permit. For example, if a storm ends at 2 P.M., the climber can then start to climb; farther south, this day would be lost for climbing.

Before May 15 and after August 1, there are at least three hours of total darkness. Outside of this date range, storms will upset climbing schedules because the opportunity to climb throughout the night will not exist.

Prevailing Weather Trends The prevailing winds are south and southwest off the ocean. The prevailing wind from the ocean usually carries warm air. When this warm air hits the glacier-surrounded mountains, precipitation follows. The warmer the temperature, the highter the probability of bad weather.

In the Denali area, there are likely to be a fair number of clear, but often cold and windy, days in April and early May. Although 150 miles from the ocean, Denali is unprotected from the sea to the south.

Thus, by the end of May, warm air from the ocean makes its

way to Denali and local storms develop. The weather, particularly on the southern side where the clouds often boil up, gets progressively worse after July. September is a poor month, with the highest amount of precipitation in Alaska. In February and March, there are often long periods of cold, clear weather. However, there are also violent winds from the north in winter.

Temperature Ranges It is possible for all of the big mountains to have very cold temperatures even in midsummer. Temperatures of −50 degrees have been recorded by climbers on Denali in June and July. The disadvantage of climbing in April and early May is that, in spite of more clear days, the wind blows harder and the temperatures are colder. (From December through March, temperatures drop below −40 degrees for days on end and for 24 hours at a time.)

As a rule of thumb, one can assume that the temperature will be three degrees colder for each 1,000 feet of elevation. Air temperatures during the day at 8,000 feet in June and July average around 30 degrees. The air temperature will drop five to ten degrees during the evening, although the change will seem much greater if the sun has been shining. Temperatures inside tents at midday can reach 80 degrees because of the sun.

CLEAN CLIMBING

On the West Rib, the remains of a burned out tent are visible at 15,200 feet, and human feces dot the snow both there and at the 16,500-foot campsite. In many places low on the Cassin, there are veritable tangles of old fixed line. At 16,500 feet, climbers have jettisoned excess weight from their packs; looking around in the obvious, sheltered tent site, one can find assorted hardware, a new climbing rope, a pair of long underwear, books

Crowds on the West Buttress route. *JONATHAN WATERMAN*

and various pieces of trash. Although much smaller, this site is similar to the 16,400-foot and 17,200-foot campsites on the West Buttress in that one must select cooking snow very carefully from among the wasteland of brown turds. Or, you can walk the Muldrow Glacier down low and find old canvas army tents, sardine cans and rotted clothing. Fortunately, Denali is huge, and sometimes, below 15,000 feet, snowfall will cover the excrement, the bodies, the trash and the jettisoned gear. Up high on the mountain, where the wind blows away the snow cover, there is a permanent raised sidewalk from Denali Pass to the summit. Irreversible damage has been done. Every year the number of climbers on Denali increases. Human waste disposal is a health hazard at the more popular campsites. Like the number of climbers, the damage will continue to escalate, unless climbers behave thoughtfully.

Guidelines Plan ahead about how to remove trash, food, fuel and all gear from the mountain. Expeditions prepared for every contingency, with superfluous food, gear and gas, will have a hard time getting it all down. Paper trash, such as toilet paper, can be burned, but on properly planned lightweight alpine-style climbs, it's easier to bring the trash down. All climbers should repack food and leave excess foil and paper wrappings at home. (Freeze-dried food does not spoil without foil wrappers.) Under the pretext of generosity to climbers, caches are often abandoned. However, these caches inevitably become trash dumps. Whatever supplies are carried up must be carried or dragged back down.

Dig latrine pits 18 to 24 inches deep and stake out large, heavy-duty plastic garbage bags with wands. Waste (feces, food scraps, ashes from burnt trash) can go into the bag; when the camp is broken, the bag should be thrown into the nearest crevasse. On steep routes, without crevasses, climbers must throw feces, on a snow block, away from campsite drinking snow and the route below. Fixed rope has to be pulled off the mountain after the climb. Expeditions should consult National Park Service Mountaineering Rangers about current waste problems before leaving for the mountain.

MEDICAL

Recommendations Climbers must be prepared to give medical treatment and not just first aid. It is helpful to have a doctor or an emergency medical technician in each party. At the very least, everyone should be experienced in first aid. Team members should be aware of one another's medical problems and the side effects of various drugs.

Drug Side Effects Sleeping pills are a respiratory depressant and can invite pulmonary edema. Tetracycline can increase an individual's sensitivity to the sun. Lasix is a diuretic which causes severe dehydration. Diamox is not necessary on Denali if a reasonable rate of ascent is practiced; it also causes a tingling in the extremeties that is very similar to the sensation one gets with cold fingers and toes. When preparing medical kits, climbers should consult recent high-altitude medical literature. (See Appendix I for medical kit suggestions.)

DIET

Arctic living conditions and vigorous exercise will raise the caloric demand of a climber on Denali to nearly double that of the average American. Fats (margarine, peanut butter, oil, cheese and nuts) are invaluable in combating the cold. However,

Ranger Scott Gill tending John Murphy's frostbitten feet.
JONATHAN WATERMAN

too many fats and all proteins are hard to digest, and will hinder acclimatization above 14,000 feet where a high carbohydrate diet is recommended. Six days of food should be left at base camp and 14 to 25 days of food should be carried on the climb.

Menu The expedition menu can make or break a trip. Freeze-dried food is light weight and quick to cook, but bland; a spice kit can help. At high altitude, the cooking time is longer (food sometimes has to be boiled in a pot rather than soaked), and it can be unpalatable.

There are many inexpensive dried foods (rice, pasta, cereals) that are as light as freeze-dried food, more nutritious and easy to prepare. Down low on the mountain, meat, eggs, canned fruits and cheesecake can do wonders for morale. Fresh food freezes and spoils. Some groups carry whole grains and a pressure cooker, which minimizes cooking time and fuel consumption. Regardless of the menu, spartan diets are not advised, since food becomes a central, coveted item on Denali.

Fluids Rehydration is the most important part of one's diet on Denali. Fluid loss from the body is high due to strenuous exercise in the dry air. Drinking four quarts of fluid each day can help prevent altitude sickness, exhaustion and frostbite. Caffeinated drinks are diuretics and vasoconstrictors, and will make it more difficult to withstand the cold. It's best to break the habit long before the expedition so withdrawal headaches don't hamper one's performance on the mountain. Cocoa, herbal tea, milk and soup are all fine; thermoses are marvelous for restoring energy on cold climbing days. Camelbak drinking pouches, containing 2.2 liters of water that can be sipped through a straw while climbing, are indispensable. Water and sugar drinks should be carried in a properly insulated one- to two-quart container (some climbers become dehydrated because their water freezes). Generally speaking, if the urine is not gin clear and regular, the climber is dehydrated and should be drinking more.

GROUP EQUIPMENT

Tents: The most popular, practical tent on Denali is the three-man Dome tent. For comfort, however, some parties use the high-profile McKinley tent which doesn't hold up well in high winds. Other climbers save weight and sacrifice living space by using various types of tunnel tents that stand up in high winds and are good for small bivouac sites on the steeper routes. Dark-colored tents induce depression during long storm periods. A whiskbroom and sponge are essential for cleaning out snow and spills. Most tent sites will be located on snow where ordinary snow stakes sometimes work, and where ice axes, snow pickets, flukes, wands, skis, ski poles and snowshoes all work well.

Stoves: As melting water is an essential part of a Denali climb, careful attention must be given to the choice of a stove. To minimize the possibility of tent fires and repair problems, climbers should use the stove they are most familiar with. (In 1980, a party on the West Rib had a harrowing experience when their tent burned down because they were unfamiliar with a flare-up problem on their stove.)

In order of popularity on Denali, climbers use white gas, butane, then kerosene stoves. My own preference is for Coleman multi-fuel stoves, but like any other white gas stove, it should burn near an open door (so it can be thrown out if it flares up) or outside. The Coleman is quiet, with a wide range of flame control, and seems to boil water faster than any other stove.

Some guided groups use kerosene stoves on Denali. Kerosene is not nearly as combustible or dangerous as white gas. Although the fumes can be bothersome, an inexperienced climber is less likely to torch a tent with a kerosene stove. One drawback, however, is that kerosene stoves demand more cleaning than other stoves.

A few climbers, particularly Europeans or those on technical routes, use butane/propane stoves. REI now sells a butane/propane canister that works better in the cold than the old canisters. Todd Bibler makes an excellent stove, which can be hung from the tent ceiling, and renovated with an insulated canister nest. The stove is quiet and frees up floor space. Climbers considering this type of stove must commit themselves to carrying the empty canisters back down.

With any type of stove, pocket lighters are invaluable. Insulation beneath the stove and windscreens are essential. One stove will do for up to three people. With all stoves, the hazards of tent fires and carbon monoxide poisoning from improper ventilation must be recognized.

Fuel: For kerosene or gas stoves, the minimum consumption—for freeze-dried food, not allowing any extra for burning trash—is one half pint per person per day. The minimum consumption for Butane stoves, for freeze-dried food, is one large Bluet butane canister per person for three days. A two-person team on a three-week climb would carry 13 butane canisters or three one-quart Sigg bottles with gas or kerosene. Gas and kerosene can also be carried in one-gallon, square-sided fuel containers. Fuel containers must be tested for leaks. It is important that they be kept separate from food to prevent contamination. Avoid

Coleman fuel, which has an additive that suppresses high-altitude burning performance.

Pots: Two nesting cook pots, from one and a half to two and half quarts, are recommended for each cooking group.

Ropes: The optimal climbing rope is the 165-foot, 9mm Everdry. On technical routes, climbers sometimes use 300-foot, 9mm ropes. Since 1976, the major routes on Denali have been done alpine style without using fixed ropes. Some routes are still done in the old, seige style and, unfortunately, abandoned ropes and hardware often litter them. Although fixed-rope climbing allows for better acclimatization, it also entails a longer exposure to objective dangers and a considerable increase in work. The simplest solution is to consider an alpine-style ascent of a route that is within the team's abilities.

Parachute or alpine cord in 100- to 200-foot lengths is invaluable and can be used for innumerable repairs.

Snow shovels with large, sturdy aluminum scoops are essential for digging out tents during storms and for digging latrines, snow caves and cooking shelters. Plastic avalanche shovels are too small and will break.

Snow saws are needed to block walls around tents or to build igloos.

Plastic bags are always in demand. A dozen large, heavy-duty garbage bags should be carried for latrine use.

Spare parts should be considered for ice axes, crampons, tents (poles), stoves, skis, snowshoes and shovels.

225

Tool and repair kit should be carried for fixing ice axes, crampons, tents, stoves, skis, snowshoes, shovels, sleds and clothing. Such a kit might include: mechanic's wire, duct tape, hose clamps, file, crescent wrench, pliers, screwdriver, glue, wrench, and needle and thread.

Miscellaneous gear: Pot grips, scouring pads, one-quart urine bottle and toilet paper.

Thermometer authenticates the war stories when you get home.

Climbing hardware varies according to the difficulty of the route. The minimum amount, sufficient for the West Buttress or Muldrow Glacier, is one ice screw (or snow fluke) and one ice ax per person for crevasse rescue.

Radio: The National Park Service recommends that all parties carry a radio. Although there is no doubt that they have saved lives, it is not known how many parties depend on radios rather than prudence and self-sufficiency. There are, however, climbers who regard climbing Denali as a wilderness experience, in which they are isolated from the outside world and must depend only on their own resources.

Five-watt CB radios are those most commonly used. Channel 19 is monitored by the radio caretaker at the Southeast Fork of the Kahiltna, by Talkeetna glacier pilots, the National Park Service and various people living in the Alaska bush. FM transceivers are used to transmit to telephone operators in Anchorage and Fairbanks. Since there are few CB monitors on the north side of the mountain, an FM transceiver is recommended. Both CB and FM units are line-of-sight and are generally effective only above 14,000 feet. Both radios are fairly light. Several sets of batteries should be carried.

For use on routes like the Wickersham or the Northwest Buttress, there are sideband radios which can transmit nonline-of-sight or below 14,000 feet. An extra sideband radio must be left with the base camp caretaker or a bush pilot so that the party can be monitored.

Signal devices such as smoke flares, emergency locator trans-mitters and rocket flares might be carried as radio communica-tion is not always possible or desirable. There is no guarantee, however, that the weather will permit signalling. Air-to-ground signal arrangements should be made with the Park Service or pilots.

PERSONAL EQUIPMENT

Boots: Loose-fitting double boots work best with crampons, although some climbers use floppy vapor barrier (mouse) boots, which don't hold crampons as well and trap all moisture.

Overboots are needed for most double boots. They must be well insulated in the sole.

Gaitors are essential on vapor barrier boots; for double boots, they are useful when down low on the mountain.

Twelve-point crampons must fit snugly with allowance for over-boots. Strapless (Footfang) or cable-binding crampons are best.

Socks: At least two changes of wool socks should be carried.

Vapor barrier socks can reduce the number of wool socks carried. Both socks and feet must be dried every night to prevent immersion foot.

T-shirt: This is useful on the hot glaciers below 10,000 feet.

Capilene underwear takes perspiration away from the skin to the next layer of clothing. Tops and bottoms are suggested.

Expedition underwear: Wool, Damart or Patagonia tops and bottoms all work well.

Mountain pants: Pile, wool, thinsulate or fiberfill pants should be ankle length.

Wind pants: Gore-Tex is best, although regular, breathable nylon will work too. Bibs are warmer and keep the snow out better.

Hooded windjacket should be Gore-Tex and fit loosely.

Pile jacket is indispensable and works well as a pillow.

Hooded down jacket is great around camp, on bivouacs or on summit days.

Wool shirt can be worn underneath the pile jacket.

Patagonia capilene gloves seem to outwear any other gloves. Bring two pair.

228

Roger Mear dressed for his winter climb of the Cassin Ridge.
JONATHAN WATERMAN

Helly Hansen pile or Dachstein wool mittens dry out quicker than any other mittens. Bring two pair.

Overmittens are essential; Gore-Tex or Cordura. Idiot straps or clip-ons prevent the mittens from getting lost.

Balaclava made out of pile or wool is essential.

Silk mask is nice when it gets very cold. Good for breathing through to protect lungs on cold days.

Spare wool hat should be carried for each party.

Face masks with eye slits tend to blind the wearer. Half-neoprene ski Masques work well in conjunction with goggles.

Double lens goggles work well in blowing snow conditions, but are prone to fogging. Only lenses that screen out untraviolet light should be used.

Mountaineering glasses should screen out at least ninety percent of the ultraviolet light radiation. Side shields are okay, but will often fog up. A spare pair of glasses should be carried for each group.

Visored cap is important for sun protection.

Water bottle should have a one- to two-quart capacity. Water will freeze if the bottle is not properly insulated.

Pack with soft internal frame is preferred by most climbers, although heavier loads are easier to carry with an external pack frame, which makes technical climbing or skiing awkward.

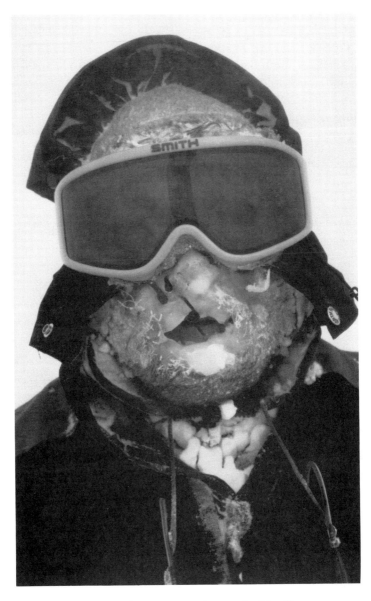

Climber in stormy weather at 11,000 feet on the West Buttress.
BRIAN OKONEK

Ice ax should have a safety strap (attached to the wrist or harness), otherwise a spare ax should be carried. Technical routes demand an ax shorter than 70 centimeters. For the Muldrow or West Buttress routes an ax under 65 centimeters would be too short.

Helmets are necessary only on technical routes.

Ascenders, such as Jumars, Clogs or Gibbs, are mandatory and should be attached to the rope at all times.

Ice screw or snow fluke, either one or both, should be carried by each climber for crevasse rescue.

Climbing harness is essential. Consider a chest harness too.

Sleeping bags made of fiberfill or down both work well. Fiberfill is heavier than down, but is preferable for warmth when wet. Although there are usually enough sunny days to dry out a Gore-Tex down sleeping bag, it should be used with a bivouac cover.

Vapor barrier liner can add ten degrees of warmth to the sleeping bag as well as keeping it dry. It is inexpensive, lighweight and very clammy.

Sleeping pad must be at least one-half inch thick; some climbers carry two. It is important to get a brand that will not freeze and break in the cold. Therm-a-Rests are great, but a puncture would be a let down. Without a pad, a sleeping bag is nearly useless.

Skis or snowshoes speed glacier travel, which would be much slower and more dangerous without them. Skins are recommended for skis. Sherpa and Red Feather brand snowshoes are light and sturdy.

Sled or haul bag inside a tube tent makes transporting gear on a glacier much easier than if it were all carried inside a pack. Sleds will tip over unless they are expensive, custom-made models. Cheap plastic tube tents covering a haul bag work great. Fasten the tube tent at both ends, like a giant sausage, then tie the dragline into a swivel gate attached to the haul bag. The tube tent can roll over sideways without having to be righted and without tangling the rope.

Pocket knife is invaluable.

Eating bowl, cup and spoon, as well as journal, pencil, camera and film, are other important items to carry.

Books and other reading material become quite popular during bad weather. Each book should be of general interest reading. Books emphasizing sex and violence always seem to be popular.

233

C H A P T E R

The *Use* of *Drugs* at *High Altitudes*

by

Peter H. Hackett, M.D.

he increasing sophistication of modern mountain- eering extends not only to shelters, clothing, and hardware, but also to medicine, especially that involving the treatment of high-altitude illness.

Severe altitude illness must be considered an objective hazard of high-altitude mountaineering, particularly on alpine and "superalpine" climbs. Climbers should know how to optimize the chances of survival in such situations. The tragic deaths of competent physician-climbers, such as Chris Chandler (on Kangchenjunga) and Pete Thexton (on Broad Peak), emphasize the abrupt and deadly nature of altitude illness, even for those with medical training.

The traditional method of going down at the first sign of altitude illness is still the safest course of action. But immediate descent is not always an option. Medication can be used to treat altitude-related conditions, making quick descents less critical.

The recently marketed hyperbaric (Gamow) bag is one temporary solution for critically sick climbers. The equivalent of a

5,000–foot descent can be made by enclosing the victim in this eight-pound fabric bag and pressurizing it. This may allow the climber adequate recovery to then descend safely.

Some mountaineers use medication to prevent high-altitude illness, while others use it to optimize their performance. Still others eschew the use of drugs altogether. This may be an appropriate philosophical choice, but could also increase the chance of dying if severe high-altitude illness were to strike. Such decisions should be made with full awareness of the risks.

OXYGEN

Oxygen is the most useful agent in the treatment of high-altitude illness. Little, if any, evidence exists that climbing to extreme altitude causes long-term brain damage. Impairments in cerebral function, such as recent memory loss and problems with speech and mentation, have all been shown to reverse with descent.

Oxygen is the most effective agent for the treatment of high-altitude illness. Useful for any degree of illness, it can be lifesaving in high-altitude pulmonary edema. The body cannot store oxygen very well, so that oxygen breathing is only effective while it is being used; full recovery from HAPE, for example, may take more than 24 hours of oxygen therapy, and adequate supplies are rarely available. So oxygen is generally used to buy time while arranging a descent or evacuation, or as a lifesaving measure. Any amount of oxygen is helpful in high-altitude illness. When supplies are limited, it is given at a low flow rate (½ to 2 liters per minute) in order to prolong its use. A common misconception is that a climber's condition may become worse if oxygen is started and then runs out. Oxygen is helpful for the period of its use, and if used for more than a few hours, it may

Dr. Peter Hackett in the medical camp tent at 14,300 feet.
JONATHAN WATERMAN

have a lasting effect, just as descent for a few hours may be helpful. When sudden, severe high-altitude illness strikes, oxygen may be the only hope of survival.

Acetazolalmide (diamox)

Effects: Diamox inhibits an enzyme called carbonic anhydrase. Otherwise, the enzyme helps carbon dioxide dissolve in body fluids, where it is carried to the lung and breathed out as a gas. The enzyme also regulates kidney functions, thereby changing the acid-base balance of the body.

When the enzyme is blocked by Diamox, the kidney excretes more bicarbonate, causing the user to urinate. The blood becomes more acid and counteracts the body's usual alkalotic state at high altitude, which causes an increase in the volume of air moved by the lungs, and a higher blood oxygen level.

A climber with a higher oxygen level is physiologically at a lower altitude. Breathing becomes more regular, especially during the night, which abolishes periodic or Cheyne—Stokes breathing. The dumping of bicarbonate by the kidney and increased breathing is effected by Diamox within a few hours; without Diamox, the process normally takes as long as four days.

Side Effects and Risk/Benefit Ratio: One common side effect of Diamox is tingling of the skin, usually in the extremities and face (although it can occur anywhere, sometimes humorously so). This can be reduced by decreasing the dosage.

Nearly everyone notices increased urination, expecially during their first days on the drug. Persons using Diamox are advised to keep a large urine receptacle in thier tent. The increased urination may cause mild dehydration, so drink extra fluid while using Diamox.

Some people develop nausea and vomiting or drowsiness after taking the drug. Another less-frequently reported side effect is a change in vision, especially in a myopic person. Also, since CO^2 is not instantly hydrated on the tongue, Diamox allows you to taste the CO^2 in carbonated beverages (including beer), ruining the flavor, and producing a tingling sensation on the tongue.

Although the side effects are not serious, they can have major consequences. For instance, during the first ascent of Cholatse, we climbed from 16,000 to 19,000 feet. Although I had been feeling well and going strong, I thought that Diamox would improve my safety after such a large altitude gain. I took a 250 mg tablet that evening. I was nauseated all night, and in the morning vomited my dinner.

I couldn't tell if this was a side effect of Diamox or the onset of altitude illness, and decided that rather than slowing down everyone else, I should stay behind. The other four made it to the summit and back to camp. Since I recovered quickly, I had probably experienced a side effect from the Diamox.

The main, albeit uncommon, risk of this sulfa drug is developing an allergy. Symptoms could include rashes, nausea, wheezing, or more rarely, life-threatening shock. Anyone with sulfa sensitivity should not take Diamox. Otherwise, climbers should try the drug at home before using it on a peak, although such a test is no guarantee.

Usage: Some experts, especially English physicians, recommend that Diamox be taken by everyone ascending to high altitude in order to prevent altitude illness, and possibly to improve physical performance. Other experts do not agreee, since the drug is not necessary for most people, and feel that the emphasis should be on proper acclimatization rather than protection from a drug.

At a recent meeting of the International Mountain Medicine Society in Switzerland, a panel of experts generally agreed on the following usage: 1) For prevention of altitude illness in persons with susceptibility to acute mountain sickness and HAPE, in conjunction with gradual ascent. 2) For those who must make a rapid ascent to altitude, without adequate time for acclimatization. This includes climbers or trekkers flying directly from sea level to Lhasa, Cuzco, La Paz, and other high-altitude locations. It is also recommended for abrupt ascent for high-altitude rescues. 3) To speed acclimatization and abort symptoms of early mountain sickness. The drug can be quite effective when given early in the course of altitude illness. 4) For treatment of severe periodic breathing that results in poor sleep and frequent wakening with the feeling of suffocation.

Dosage: The drug is powerful, and does not have to be taken in large doses, which cause more side effects. For prevention and treatment, dosage is the same.

Average-sized adult males should take one 250 mg tablet twice a day (once in the morning and once in the evening), or a single 500 mg sustained-action capsule once every 24 hours. For women, smaller males, and adolescents, 125 mg twice a day is adequate. The dosage in children is smaller, depending on body weight. For treatment of periodic breathing, one tablet of 125 or 250 mg at dinner time is sufficient. New information indicates that even smaller doses may be just as effective and cause fewer side effects.

For prevention, the drug should be started 24 hours prior to ascent to altitude and continued for the first day or two at

242

altitude. It can then be discontinued, and not restarted unless symptoms of mountain sickness (headaches, nausea, dizziness, lassitude) start to develop.

For treatment, the drug should be continued for 24–48 hours, or until symptoms disappear. The physiologic actions of the drug persist for at least two days after stopping it. Even though the drug is no longer in the blood, the kidneys must reaccumulate the lost bicarbonate.

A common misconception is that Diamox masks the symptoms of serious altitude illness. This is incorrect. The drug acts by improving acclimatization and counteracting the causes of mountain sickness, which include fluid retention, inadequate breathing, and other factors. Therefore, Diamox does not mask the problem, but treats the cause.

Diamox does not work in all cases of altitude sickness. People cannot take Diamox and then overstep the limits of their ability to acclimatize. For example, Galen Rowell developed HAPE while using Diamox, after climbing from 9,000 to 20,000 feet in ten hours. Diamox did not mask Rowell's HAPE, which developed despite the Diamox because of his rapid rate of ascent.

Experience with the drug at extreme altitude is quite limited. There is no question of its value at altitudes up to 18,000 feet; beyond that, the drug may not be as useful.

For example, on the 1981 American Medical Expedition to Mount Everest, Diamox was not effective in treating altitude illness, as it usually is at lower altitudes. Also, the effect of Diamox on exercise performance is unclear. Based on present evidence, the drug should not be used in hopes of improving exercise performance. Of course, performance will increase if climbers are not suffering from altitude illness.

Climbers descending Karsten's Ridge, Muldrow Glacier.
JONATHAN WATERMAN

Dexamethasone (Decadron)

Effects: The action of Decadron is a bit mysterious. It is a steroid, but not for body-building. This type of steroid prevents or treats inflammation, and is used to treat some types of brain swelling. It may prevent or treat the brain swelling from altitude illness, and reduce symptoms, but there are other actions as well. It reduces nausea and vomiting in cancer patients, and it may also do this at high altitude. Also, the drug produces a heightened sense of well-being which may make persons at altitude feel better.

Decadron will also not mask symptoms of altitude illness. The drug effectively treats symptoms of acute mountain sickness, but unlike Diamox, it does not improve the natural processes of acclimatization. As a result, if the drug is discontinued before acclimatization takes place, illness may develop. This is the major drawback in its use for prevention. So far, Decadron has only been beneficial for cerebral symptoms, and not for HAPE.

Side Effects and Risks/Benefits: Side effects of Decadron depend on the length of time it is used. A single dose is essentially without significant side effects. For short-term use, side effects include a change in mood (such as euphoria or anxiety or restlessness), more interesting or even bizarre dreams, and perhaps increased sexual arousal. A feeling of an unsettled stomach is common, and sometimes nausea develops. Some persons complain of hyperacidity and heartburn.

If used for two or more days, serious side effects can possibly develop (but rarely). Most noticeably, when the drug is used for this length of time, and then suddenly withdrawn, feelings of

246

depression can be severe. Even as a single dose wears off, one can often feel the euphoria change to slight depression.

When the drug is taken for prevention, these mood swings are especially noticeable. More importantly, as the drug wears off, so does the protection from altitude hypoxia (lack of oxygen). Symptoms, such as dizziness and headaches, may rapidly progress if the Decadron is stopped too soon after ascent. When the drug is taken to treat symptoms of altitude illness, the victim's improvement overshadows the minor side effects.

Allergy to Decadron is so rare as to not be a real consideration. Persons with a history of ulcer disease or hyperacidity are more likely to develop the gastrointestinal symptoms. Persons with a history of psychiatric illness should also be careful with Decadron. Rarely, a full-blown psychotic episode, or "nervous breakdown," can develop, which could be a real catastrophe on a mountaineering expedition. So far, this has not been reported in climbers taking the drug.

Usage: The use of Decadron for altitude illness is still relatively new and continuing to evolve. At this time, most experts agree that the drug should be reserved for treatment of moderate to severe altitude illness, and not used for prevention, except in those allergic to Diamox, and only if chemical prevention is truly necessary. The drug should definitely be given to climbers at altitude who develop loss of coordination (ataxia) and change in consciousness. These symptoms usually develop in climbers who have already contracted acute mountain sickness (headache, nausea or vomiting, trouble sleeping, and lassitude), or HAPE (shortness of breath, weakness, cough, and lung congestion).

Decadron should be given to anyone who becomes uncon-

247

scious from altitude illness, although it may be too late to be of much help. Sometimes, however, the only symptoms of severe altitude sickness may be trouble with coordination and/or mental changes. In the presence of either of these two symptoms, Decadron should be administered and the climber should be taken down immediately, preferably with oxygen. In the event that descent has to be delayed, Decadron may make a critical difference.

Another usage is for persistent nausea and vomiting. Injectable Decadron works much better than Diamox for this purpose, and perhaps as well as Compazine or similar antivomiting drugs.

Recently, climbers have been using Decadron as "protection" during alpine-style ascents, which is not medically prudent. Persons particularly susceptible to altitude illness, however, may be an exception. Steve Boyer (a physician-climber), who has been stricken by recurrent bouts of HAPE on Himalayan peaks, has discovered that after taking Decadron, he can do alpine pushes to extreme altitude without illness.

There is no scientific evidence that Decadron improves physical performance at altitude, and it should not be taken for this purpose. Because Decadron is so effective in treating moderate to severe altitude illness, it shoud be carried in all high-altitude medical kits.

An argument could be made for using Diamox and Decadron together, since Diamox speeds acclimatization and has a longer effect, and Decadron treats the acute symptoms. In fact, this has been done on Denali a number of times, but only when descent was not possible. Someone ill enough to require Decadron should probably descend.

Dosage: For both prevention and treatment, ingesting 4 mg of Decadron every six hours has been shown to be effective. One study reported good results for treatment of altitude illness with 8 mg initially, followed by 4 mg every six hours. The drug can be injected into a vein or muscle, or it can be taken orally if the climber is not vomiting. It should be continued until the victim reaches a lower altitude or all symptoms have disappeared.

However, if treatment was for more than 24 hours, Decadron should be reduced gradually to 2 mg every six hours for four doses. If symptoms of acute mountain sickness recur, a full dose (4 mg every six hours) should be reinstituted until the victim can be moved to a lower altitude.

OTHER DRUGS

A few other drugs are also useful at high altitude. One is a decongestant nasal spray (Afrin, for example), which relieves the high-altitude stuffy nose. During the night, nasal congestion forces mouth breathing, resulting in severly dried and sore throats. On the Everest medical expedition, Afrin was the single most requested item from the medical kit.

Antiemetics, such as Compazine (prochlorperazine) and Phenergan (promethazine) are useful for the nausea and vomiting of altitude illness, but do not cure acute mountain sickness. Specific details of their use can be obtained from a physician.

Sleeping pills, although popular, are best avoided because of the potential depression of respiration, which can worsen or bring on altitude illness. If a sleeping medication seems necessary, use Diamox, since the interruption in sleep may be due to periodic breathing.

APPENDICES

APPENDIX A

NUMBER OF CLIMBERS
ATTEMPTING DENALI
1903–1990

YEARS	NUMBER OF CLIMBERS	REACHED SUMMIT
1903–1912	42	0
1913–1922	4	4
1923–1932	13	4
1933–1942	18	7
1943–1952	44	21
1953–1962	167	98
1963–1972	802	406
1973–1977	1715	1001
1978–1982	2959	1535
1983–1987	3621	1776
1988–1990	2923	1659
88-YEAR TOTAL	12308	6511

APPENDIX B

FATALITY RATES ON DENALI
1903–1990

CATEGORY	NUMBER OF CLIMBERS	PERCENT
ASCENT	28	43.75
DESCENT	36	56.25

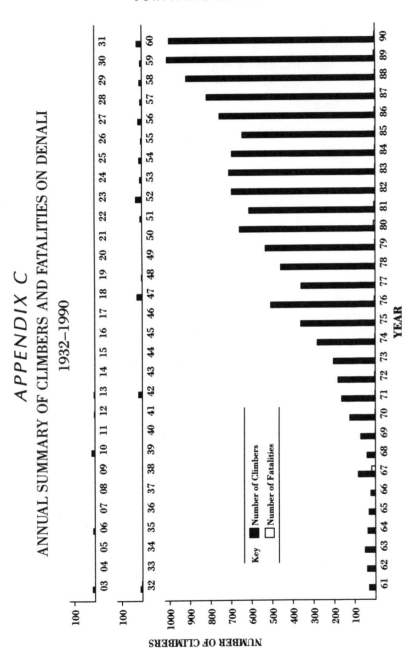

APPENDIX C

ANNUAL SUMMARY OF CLIMBERS AND FATALITIES ON DENALI

1932–1990

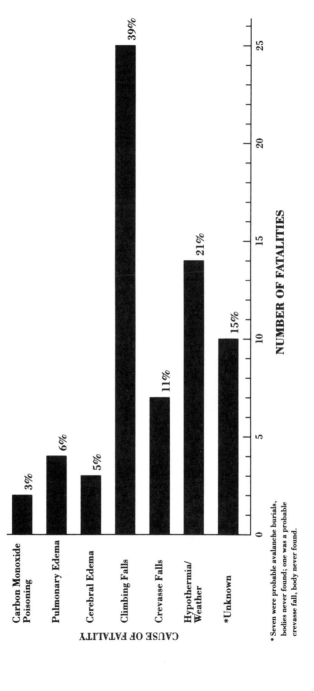

APPENDIX D
FATALITIES ON DENALI
1903–1990

CAUSE OF FATALITY

- Carbon Monoxide Poisoning — 3%
- Pulmonary Edema — 6%
- Cerebral Edema — 5%
- Climbing Falls — 39%
- Crevasse Falls — 11%
- Hypothermia/Weather — 21%
- *Unknown — 15%

NUMBER OF FATALITIES

0   5   10   15   20   25

* Seven were probable avalanche burials, bodies never found; one was a probable crevasse fall, body never found.

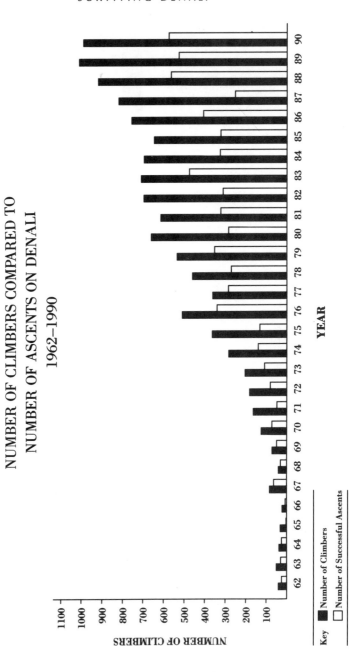

APPENDIX E

NUMBER OF CLIMBERS COMPARED TO
NUMBER OF ASCENTS ON DENALI
1962–1990

Key ■ Number of Climbers
     □ Number of Successful Ascents

SURVIVING DENALI

APPENDIX F

GUIDE SERVICES AUTHORIZED
TO OPERATE IN
DENALI NATIONAL PARK AND PRESERVE

Alaska Denali Guiding
P.O. Box 556
Talkeetna, Alaska 99676
907-733-2649

Genet Expeditions
Building D
4602 Business Park Boulevard
Anchorage, Alaska 99503
800-334-3638, 907-561-2123

American Alpine Institute
1212 24th Street
Bellingham, Washington 98225
206-671-1505

Fantasy Ridge Mountain Guides
P.O. Box 1679
Telluride, Colorado 81435
303-728-3546

Mountain Trip
P.O. Box 91161
Anchorage, Alaska 99509
907-345-6499

Rainier Mountaineering, Inc.
535 Dock Street–209
Tacoma, Washington 98402
206-627-6242

National Outdoor Leadership School
P.O. Box AA
Lander, Wyoming 82520
307-332-6973

APPENDIX G

INFORMATION SOURCES
FOR EXPEDITIONS TO DENALI

Journals
ACCIDENTS IN NORTH AMERICAN MOUNTAINEERING
THE AMERICAN ALPINE JOURNAL
The American Alpine Club
113 East 90th Street
New York, New York 10128-1589

THE CANADIAN ALPINE JOURNAL
The Alpine Club of Canada
P.O. Box 1026
Banff, Alberta T0L 0C0
Canada

THE MOUNTAIN WORLD
Published by the Swiss Foundation for Alpine Research from 1953 to
1969. Collections available for reference in the library of The American Alpine Club and several other libraries which have mountaineering
collections.

Magazines
CLIMBING
P.O. Box 339
Carbondale, Colorado 81623

MOUNTAIN
P.O. Box 184
Sheffield S11 9DL
England

258

ROCK & ICE
P.O. Box 3595
Boulder, Colorado 80306

SUMMIT
111 Schweitz Road
Fleetwood, Pennsylvania 19522

Map

University of Alaska Press
1st Floor Gruening Building
University of Alaska Fairbanks
Fairbanks, Alaska 99775-1580

Photographs

Museum of Science
Attention: Bradford Washburn
Science Park
Boston, Massachusetts 02114

Expedition Information

Denali National Park and Preserve
P.O. Box 588
Talkeetna, Alaska 99676

APPENDIX H

DENALI
APPROACH SERVICES

Air Service
The following air services will fly climbers to Denali:

Doug Geeting Aviation
P.O. Box 42
Talkeetna, Alaska 99676
907-733-2366

Hudson Air Service, Inc.
P.O. Box 82
Talkeetna, Alaska 99676
907-733-2321

K2 Aviation
P.O. Box 545
Talkeetna, Alaska 99676
907-733-2291

Talkeetna Air Taxi
P.O. Box 73
Talkeetna, Alaska 99676
907-733-2218

Dog Sled Service (Denali North Side)
Denali Dog Tours
P.O. Box 30
Denali National Park, Alaska 99755

APPENDIX I

MEDICAL KIT SUGGESTIONS
FOR EXPEDITIONS TO DENALI
(See Chapter 10)

ITEM	USE
ADVIL	MILD HEADACHE
AFRIN	NASAL CONGESTION
CODEINE	PAINKILLER
CORICIDIN	FOR COLDS
DECADRON	SEVERE AMS OR HACE
DEMEROL	STRONG PAINKILLER
DIAMOX	POSSIBLE AMS PREVENTION
HEMORRHOID OINTMENT	HEMORRHOID INFLAMMATION
KEFLEX	ANTIBIOTIC
LABIOSAN	LIP PROTECTION
LOMOTIL	DIARRHEA
OIL OF CLOVES	TOOTHACHE
SUNBLOCK	SUNBURN PREVENTION
THROAT LOZENGES	SORE THROAT

Additional items which might be included:

GAUZE	SUTURE KIT
COMPRESSES	ADHESIVE TAPE
RECTAL THERMOMETER	SPARE SUNGLASSES

Two books are recommended as valuable field guides:

Mountain Sickness, by Peter H. Hackett, M.D.,
   The American Alpine Club, New York

Medicine for Mountaineering, by James A. Wilkerson, M.D.,
   The Mountaineers, Seattle

BIBLIOGRAPHY

Davidson, Art. *Minus 148°: The Winter Ascent of Mt. McKinley*. Second, Enlarged Edition. Cloudcap Press, Seattle, 1986.

Freedman, Lewis. *Dangerous Steps: Vernon Tejas and the Solo Winter Ascent of Denali*. Stackpole Books, Harrisburg, 1990.

Hackett, Peter H. *Mountain Sickness: Prevention, Recognition & Treatment*. The American Alpine Club, New York, 1980.

Heath, Donald and David Reid Williams. *Man at High Altitude: The Pathophysiology of Acclimatization and Adaption*. Churchill Livingstone, Edinburgh, 1977.

Houston, Charles S. *Going Higher: The Story of Man and Altitude*. Third Edition, Revised. Little, Brown and Company, Boston, 1987.

Jones, Chris. *Climbing in North America*. University of California Press, Berkeley, and The American Alpine Club, New York, 1976.

Mills, W. J. "Frostbite and Hypothermia," *Alaska Medicine*, March 1973.

Moore, Terris. *Mt. McKinley: The Pioneer Climbs*. The Mountaineers, Seattle, 1981.

Mountaineering: Denali National Park and Preserve, Alaska. National Park Service, U.S. Department of the Interior, 1987.

Perla, Ronald I. and M. Martinelli, Jr. *Avalanche Handbook*. Agriculture Handbook 489. Forest Service, U.S. Department of Agriculture, Fort Collins (Colorado), 1976.

Selters, Andy. *Glacier Travel and Crevasse Rescue*. The Mountaineers, Seattle, 1990.

Sherwonit, Bill. *To the Top of Denali*. Alaska Northwest Books, Seattle, 1990.

Snyder, Howard H. *The Hall of the Mountain King*. Charles Scribner's Sons, New York, 1973.

Stuck, Hudson. *The Ascent of Denali (Mount McKinley): A Narrative of the First Complete Ascent of the Highest Peak in North America*. Charles Scribner's Sons, New York, 1914.

Washburn, Bradford. "Frostbite," *The American Alpine Journal 1962*.

Washburn, Bradford and David Roberts. *Mount McKinley: The Conquest of Denali*. Harry N. Abrams, New York, 1991.

Waterman, Jonathan. *High Alaska: A Historical Guide to Denali, Foraker, and Hunter*. The American Alpine Club, New York, 1989.

Wilcox, Joe. *White Winds*. Hwong Publishing Company, Los Alamitos (California), 1981.

Wilkerson, James A., editor. *Medicine for Mountaineering*. Third Edition. The Mountaineers, Seattle, 1975.

Wilson, Rodman *et al*. "Death on Denali," *Western Journal of Medicine*, June 1978.